"You're Kidding, Right?"

*OH NO, NOT ANOTHER
BOOK ON HOW TO MAKE
MONEY INVESTING IN
STOCKS AND BONDS*

Brad Goldfarb, CIMA®

Fulton Books, Inc.
Meadville, PA

First originally published by Fulton Books 2020

ISBN 978-1-64654-655-8 (Paperback)
ISBN 978-1-64654-657-2 (Hardcover)
ISBN 978-1-64654-656-5 (Digital)

Printed in the United States of America

This book is dedicated to my wife, Patti, and our children—
Drew, Alex & Kelsey, and Samantha—who always encouraged
me and kept me moving forward with unconditional love.
Without them, my success would have only been a dream.

Why I Wrote This Book

Let me be clear, this book does not offer or even attempt to give advice on how to make money by investing in stocks and bonds. Actually, it's quite the opposite. It's a book on what to avoid and on not allowing your emotions to dictate your investment decisions. I'm not even going to discuss individual stocks, but rather pooled investments like ETFs (Exchange Traded Funds) and mutual funds, which I feel are much safer and diversified.

I provide clarity and understanding on methods of complex analysis and investing in simplistic terms to help you make better decisions. This book is not intended to take the place of using a qualified and skilled financial advisor. However, it should help you work with an advisor better by understanding these concepts.

I have to admit, I am not a major fan of books that ramble on for a ridiculous number of pages just to tell you how to "screw in a light bulb," which could have been written in a single paragraph. With that said, I promise to be brief and succinct in just a few short pages for each chapter. Don't worry, there is no test at the end, so just enjoy the ride and take in what you want. There is no need to understand the analytics behind the equation—I couldn't be happier that computers do the calculations for us. I think it is more important to just understand what things mean so you can use the knowledge in a practical way.

This book originally was created out of the humor I found in some of the things clients and prospects said to me. That's why I called it *You're Kidding, Right?*. It was the only response I could have to these questions at the time. It was a few years later that I realized all these questions were really about behavioral finance and the emotional thoughts behind their decisions. Let's be honest, we have all thought these questions, but not many had the guts to ask them. Similar to being in a classroom (possibly sitting in the back of the room and allowing all the geeks and nerds with their pocket protectors and calculators to sit up front), where you had a question for the teacher but were afraid of sounding stupid, so you never asked it. Then one of the kids in the front of the class (probably wearing glasses with very thick lenses and tape over the bridge) raised their hand and asked the very same question you thought. When the teacher said, "Johnny, that's a great question," you immediately thought that was your question and should have gotten the credit. Basically, all the questions in section 2 are those we all thought at one time or another but only a few had the guts to ask.

Prior to my retirement, I worked with many of the financial advisor trainees to teach them some of the skills I learned when I studied for my CIMA® designation in 1996—advanced analytic skills and tools I used daily in my practice as an advisor and portfolio manager. I streamlined the various topics so they would be easy to understand and they could present them to their prospective clients in a meaningful way without being condescending. And section 3 was born!

My beliefs are that too many investors don't make money because of a few things:

- They do not have defined goals
- They do not fully understand risk (or know what their own definition of risk is)
- The expectations are out of line with their risk tolerance
- They do not understand what investing long term really means
- They use emotions and/or instincts to make decisions (usually wrong)
- They are too intimidated by what they perceive as complex strategies

I hope this book will provide answers to all these issues and provide you with the success you are seeking to manage your investments. Try not to overcomplicate, and most importantly, stay the course no matter how tough things may seem.

Contents

Section 3   The Mystery Solved for Analysis and Investing: Just the Facts

- Expectations
  - Historical Returns
  - What Is Real Rate of Return?
  - The 1980s and the Introduction of No-Load Mutual Funds
  - Why Many Investors Lose Money?
  - Behavioral Finance
  - What Is Long-Term Investing?
  - Choosing the Proper Level of Risk in the Beginning
- The Dow and the S&P 500 (How Diversified Are They?)
  - What Is Cap Weighting?

- Equity ETFs
- Bond (Fixed Income) ETFs
  - Quality Rating
  - Default Rates
- What Does Long and Short Mean?
- Leveraged ETFs
- Inverse ETFs (Dangers, Especially Leveraged Inverse ETFs)

- Mutual Funds
- Bond Funds
    - Risks in a Rising Interest Rate Environment
    - Benefits in a Declining Interest Rate Environment
    - What Duration Means and How to Use It
- Equity Funds
- Hidden Costs to Be Aware Of
- The Main Differences Between ETFs and Mutual Funds

- Some Thoughts to Ponder
- What Is Modern Portfolio Theory (MPT)?
- Are You a Fiduciary? (If You Are,
  This Is Extremely Important)
- Diversification
    - Styles and Classes
    - Risky Assets vs. Riskless Assets
    - Can You Diversify Away Risk?
    - Choosing Styles
- Investing via Momentum (Style Shifts and Style Rotation)

- What Is Expected Return?
- What Is Standard Deviation?
    - Calculating Expected Ranges of Returns Using
      Standard Deviation Using a Bell Curve
- What is a P/E Ratio?

Section 1
Behavioral Finance

Chapter 1

The Mystery Behind Behavioral Finance and Emotional Investing?

Rational decision-making is how you should act during times of risk or euphoria in the stock market, but behavioral finance is the study of how investors actually react during these times—and is usually wrong!

Investing on emotion rather than being rational is very real. Just ask yourself (and he honest), At severe downturns in the market like the crash of 1987, the bottom of the tech bubble in March 2003, or the bottom of the financial crises on March 9, 2009, did you really want to add more funds to the stock market? If you are really honest, you have to say no, unless you are Warren Buffett who always thinks long term and, ironically, is always right. I'll admit it, during those times, I was scared and didn't invest more of my own money or advise clients to add funds. We are all emotional when it comes to things like this, so just admit it.

They say the definition of *stupidity* is "doing the same wrong things over and over but looking for a different outcome each time."

When it comes to investing your hard-earned money, it sounds easy on paper to do the right thing, but in reality, we act on our emotions rather than being rational. And we typically make the wrong decisions.

Too many also treat investing like gambling, which is a major mistake. It's not gambling! Long term is not an hour, day, week, or month after you invest your funds. You shouldn't get in and out and try to time the financial markets. Maybe this is a bad analogy, but if you are married and every time you had an argument with your spouse you filed for divorce, you would probably spend most of your life in court. Disagreements and down cycles are a part of life, so get over it. Instead, evaluate the situation, maybe make a few adjustments, and stay with it (in section 3, we will discuss diversification).

The way I have explained to clients over the years how to handle your portfolio is to think about it like a business. You, the investor, is chairman of the board. Your financial advisor is your chief financial officer. Like any business, your goal is to be profitable. However, all businesses go through cycles, and during downtrends, you want to be able to keep your nose above water and survive so you are there for the good times (that, too, involves proper diversity and sophisticated management techniques we will discuss in section 3). Think of it this way: by investing in stocks, you are investing in many companies with proven management and proven track records. Why invest 1 million dollars or so to buy a McDonald's franchise (if you can even get one) when you can buy shares of the entire company? This way, if an individual store goes under, it's not a major impact on the share price. Plus you don't have to run the company. At the end of the day (or years), you are looking for a return on your capital.

Let's look at a chart of the cycle of market emotions (below). I will run through a very basic but real scenario that happens to many.

Your advisor suggests buying something (or adding funds to your professionally managed portfolio). Maybe you are around the hope part of the cycle and say, "Let me think about it." You have the conversation a few more times over the next few weeks, but you still cannot decide. Somewhere around excitement part, you agree and go in. For a short while, you feel so good and are glad you waited, until the markets go through a downturn and you face anxiety or fear, and your nerves kick in. Typically, around capitulation or depression, you realize investing is not for you, and you sell because you are panicked, only to realize your mistake as things turn around and you go back in around optimistic only to start the cycle again (and again).

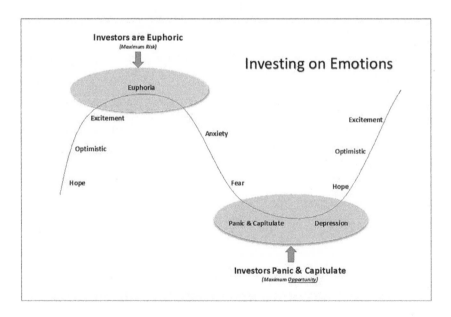

Think like Warren Buffett for a moment. He is just the opposite. He finds opportunities and value because he is a long-term investor.

It's not that he doesn't make mistakes—he does. But that's why it's also so important to have good diversity and not have all your money in one investment.

Time for another analogy to make my point: Two people walk into a room filled with horse manure, and it smells awful! While one is complaining about the stench and cannot wait to get out of the room, the other boastfully says, "There's a pony in here somewhere, and I'm going to find it!" The point is not to be so anxious to leave.

It's not about being an optimist. You shouldn't stay with a bad investment or even a bad advisor. But evaluate why things are the way they are before you make the changes. Many times, you will find nothing is really wrong and it's just part of the cycle. In baseball, if you get a hit only one out of every three at bats, you are an MVP and considered amazing (although I wouldn't want a surgeon to operate on me with those odds).

I once heard that "there will always be a part of your portfolio you will love and another part you will hate." That's what diversity is all about. Like baseball, every batter is not expected to get a homerun (batters 1 and 2 are just looking to get a hit, so batters 3, 4, and 5 can swing away to bring them home; and the last batter, usually the pitcher, is generally thankful he can pitch so he can keep his job).

*****

Now for the dull and boring part of this book (*disclaimer*: If you aren't a history buff and you want to avoid falling asleep, just skip to section 2 and chapter 2. If you choose to continue reading this part, please do not operate heavy machinery while reading).

The origin of behavioral finance dates back to Selden's 1912 *Psychology of the Stock Market*, but the official beginning was 1979, when Daniel Kahneman and Amos Tversky released *Prospect Theory: A Study of Decision Making Under Risk*.

Kahneman's study on the psychology of judgment and decision-making as well as behavioral economics was awarded a Nobel prize in Economic Sciences in 2002. With the addition of Nobel Laureates Robert Shiller (2013) and Richard Thaler (2017), numerous Nobel prizes have been awarded for behavioral research.

As we move to section 2, you will see actual quotes from my clients during my thirty-five years as an advisor, which demonstrates what behavioral finance is all about.

Section 2

Thirty-Five Years of Actual Quotes from Clients: Why I Chose the Title for This Book? You Can't Make This Stuff Up

Warning

The contents in section 2 are very real. They are from actual conversations I have had with various clients during my thirty-five-year career. Many of these quotes were said multiple times by different clients. No client names are mentioned to protect their identity (and for me to avoid a lawsuit, although I know the names of each client that made the remark).

The title of this book was the result of many of these quotes because the only way I could respond was, "You're kidding, right?" Although some of these quotes may seem ridiculous, they really are not. We are human, and this is how we think. Sometimes we speak before we realize what was said, but it's too late.

I'm sure you will relate to many of these quotes, and if you do, I hope you can use the explanations in a very constructive and positive way to avoid many of the mistakes investors typically make when their emotions get in the way of making rational decisions. Behavioral finance is very real, and the following pages are testament to it.

Chapter 2

"Nobody knows what the stock market will do"

This is very true because regardless of how brilliant people are, they just don't know with absolute certainty what tomorrow will bring. Anyone who tells you they know for certain what will happen tomorrow is either lying or totally full of themselves. Even the very best weather people are only right a percentage of the time. Things happen to change outcomes and probabilities.

John Lennon said it best in the lyrics he wrote in 1980, in a song just months before he was shot and killed: "Life is what happens to you while you're busy making other plans" ("Beautiful Boy" from John Lennon's album *Double Fantasy*).

So with that in mind, what do you do, and who do you listen to? For starters, listen to those who seem to make sense—not just because it's what you want to hear but because there is real meaning and value behind what is said or written. Just because they have a television or radio show (or write books like this) doesn't mean what they say is a fact or even remotely accurate. Just because a commentator has pearly-white large teeth and speaks with arrogance, or have their sleeves rolled up to look like they work really hard doesn't mean what they say is for you. Showmanship may be great for a show, but it's hardly personal advice. Whoever you listen to has to make sense only *to you* and be understandable in a way that is not condescending. Find advisers you relate to and who feel you can trust because they take whatever time is needed to make you comfortable without trying to sell something or rush you to sign.

You may be thinking, *Many people, even large charitable organizations, trusted Bernie Madoff, and look what happened to them.* That's true, and personally, I know quite a few people who fell for his —— and lost their entire life savings or most of it. I remember a very wealthy individual I played golf with (and knew I was a financial advisor) who bragged about his experience with Madoff saying how great and exclusive he was and how lucky he was to be using him. Side note: during my career, I never pushed business with friends or with acquaintances on the golf course, so I just said I was happy for him (I have to admit he would have been a really great client for me. But I was happy for him, but not so happy for me that he was so happy at the time). I remember him boasting (in a nice way) that his returns with Madoff every year were 10–12 percent after fees, regardless of financial market conditions. Madoff was amazing, and I couldn't or wouldn't compete with him. I chose to maintain our friendship on the golf course instead of letting business get in the way.

We didn't know it at the time, and I wouldn't second guess or question a friend who was happy with their advisor, but the keywords were "his returns every year were 10–12 percent after fees, regardless of financial market conditions." Seriously? *Seriously?* (I should type that one hundred-plus times so it sinks in and it will make this book seem longer than it is and so you will feel like you are getting something for the price you paid.)

Nobody gives away dollar bills for pennies! If someone on the street offered you a one-hundred dollar bill for ten dollars it can only be a few things:

- The one-hundred-dollar bill is real, and the person offering it to you for ten dollars is one fry short of a Happy Meal.
- It's a science experiment to see who takes it.
- It's counterfeit.

That's it! It cannot be anything else, period.

If the overall market is down, you probably will be too. Accept it. Where you find value is being down less than your chosen benchmark. You should also have a benchmark *before* you invest so you know what you are comparing to. Finding a benchmark you beat after the fact it is easy to find, and it does you no good. If you ran a mile in ten minutes but had nothing to compare it to, is it a good number? Maybe if the week before you did the same mile in four hours. Know your expectations ahead of investing (in good and bad markets), and know that markets and economies change. And although the expectations aren't a guarantee, it's a guideline to help keep you on the right course.

I remember a referral I received from a very good client. They were unhappy with every advisor they used and said they were tired of always losing money on their investments and needed someone they can trust. The couple was retired for quite a few years (they were in their seventies), and when we started talking about risk, they were emphatic that they do not want to lose money and really don't want to take much risk. They would be happy outpacing inflation so their money would last for the remainder of their lives. That seemed like an honest and fair response. I then asked, "What average return are you looking to achieve over a five- to ten-year period after fees?"

I was glad I was already sitting down as my jaw almost hit the conference room table when they told me, "We would take 12–15 percent a year after fees. *Take* 12–15 percent a year after fees… *take?* Meaning "accept"? *Seriously?* I would take next week's lottery numbers so I wouldn't have to work, but that's not happening—especially because I didn't buy a lottery ticket.

I realized they would never become clients (my choice, not theirs) when I politely asked them if they knew what the historic returns were in the stock market. They said no, and I explained that *prior to* the 2000–2002 technology bubble, it was 10 percent geometrically (compounding return) and 12 percent arithmetically (simple interest return) before fees. I quickly added that because of the severe declines in the stock market during the technology bubble in 2000–2002 and the financial crises in 2008 through early 2009, the modern-day average return is only approximately 5 percent per year. I was even more shocked when they told me that's the return they need and want (12–15 percent annually after fees), even after I explained the facts and associated risk with seeking that level of return.

I told them that the advisors they used probably managed to their desired expectations, which made their risk way too high. It was my opinion that if the advisor(s) told them what they didn't want to hear, they probably would have gone elsewhere. It's a no-win situation for the advisor, and I while I wouldn't take them as a client, not all advisors are willing to let a potential client walk out the door.

I cannot imagine how many more advisors they have had since that meeting.

Don't use an advisor just because their returns are great. Performance is *not* retroactive, and unless you are invested in insured CDs or US Treasuries, there is no guarantee. Look for an advisor who you understand and can relate to. No, you don't need to sing kumbaya together every Monday morning. Make sure their advice includes proper diversification. Having many investments is not necessarily synonymous with diversity. What if everything in the portfolio is the same asset class or style? Okay, I just got way ahead of myself—I know this is only chapter 2, and I'm not trying to impress you (yet). Don't fret. In section 3, I will cover what all this means in simple terms so you can fully understand asset allocation and work side by side with an adviser in a collaborative effort.

It's so important to know what your expectations are before doing anything, and make sure they are realistic. It's even more important to know what level of downside risk you are comfortable with and see if they go together. If they don't, I would suggest taking less risk (at least to start so you can build your confidence with what you are doing) and accept lesser returns. You can always adjust as you move forward.

Then you won't have to worry or think too much about what the markets will do going forward or who to believe.

Chapter 3

"I would have been better off the past ten years in CDs"

Hindsight is really amazing, isn't it? It allows us to be perfect. I can tell anyone what they should have done, but it's just slightly difficult to always be right about the future. But then again, even a broken clock is right twice a day.

I am willing to make a wager on who wins the 1969 World Series. Okay, I'm also a Met's fan and always have been (if you are a Yankee's fan, sorry, but it's too late to get a refund on purchasing this book, but thanks!). I'll go one step further in our wager. I'll also bet who makes the last out. For the record, it was Davey Johnson (the Met's played the Baltimore Orioles in the 1969 World Series) as he flew out to Cleon Jones in left field (Johnson later became manager of the Met's and led them to a World Series victory in 1986).

Okay, now that we covered some baseball trivia, let's get back to investing.

If the last ten years in the stock market wasn't so good or as good as you expected, then yes, you would have been better off in CDs. But since past performance is not retroactive and anyone who guarantees unusually good (or even very good) consistent returns is probably lying and you should run away from, what should you do? It all comes down to having proper expectations in both good and bad markets. Know that market returns are not linear or move in a straight line; they go up, and they go down. If you are a real investor and not a speculator, you are looking for a reasonable average return over a period of years. A real market cycle is ten years, so if you are going to invest and say, "Let's give it a shot and see what happens in a year or two," you are wasting your time and the time of those you are getting advice from. Accept down years as part of the cycle, and look at it as opportunity to add funds (if funds are available) for long-term investing.

Since everyone likes upside or good returns, you have to focus on bad years first. No, that's not being pessimistic—it's being honest and real. I don't care if you want to chant positive affirmations all day, but you need to be prepared for downturns. I remember years ago reading a quote from peak performance coach Tony Robbins, "No matter how much you look for a sunrise in the west, you aren't going to find it!" Accept the bad with the good.

Accepting that downturns are a part of the investing process is a great way to determine what level of risk you should take. In section 3, we will discuss how to evaluate risk. But for now, let's assume in a bad year, you went down as much as the benchmark you will compare to (if you are allocated 50 percent in stocks and 50 percent in fixed income, use a benchmark that is similar or the same allocation; in other words, don't compare a Ferrari Enzo to a Chevy Station Wagon. Both may be good cars, but they are very different). Are you able to stay the course? Nobody expects you to be happy or overjoyed during bad times (actually, that would be a little weird). But can you keep moving forward knowing you have a good allocation and proper diversity? Remember, the three key ingredients to success in investing are

1. buying high quality,
2. diversifying properly, and
3. duration (be a long-term investor).

I had husband-wife clients who both have MBAs in finance. When we talked about risk, they told me (in no uncertain terms), "We love risk, we eat risk, we live risk. Risk is good. After all, we have MBAs." (It was a phone conversation, so I'm not sure if when they said they had their pinkies up and eating Grey Poupon, but they do have MBAs, so let's go with that—they were very proud of it, and I did like them very much!). Well, six months after we began, the S&P 500 dropped about -10 percent (it was 1998, and a massive hedge fund, Long-Term Capital Management, almost collapsed, which could have set off a global financial crises), and the clients called me frantic and beside themselves. I quickly explained that they were down significantly less than the market after fees. It didn't matter. They were frantic and said they cannot handle the stress and need to get out right away. I went back to my notes and read them what I wrote from our phone conversation about their tolerance for risk (I even stated the date and time of that conversation). Their reaction was (and this is not an exaggeration), "We answered the questions the way we thought you wanted us to." My response was, "It doesn't matter what I think. It's not about me. It's about *you* and how *you* view risk." I couldn't make that up if I wanted to!

You should only take a level of risk you can live with at the worst of times. If you can't get through the bad times, you will never be able to stay for the good times because you will want to get out (probably somewhere around the bottom of the downturn—see section 1 for the chart on the "Cycle of Market Emotions"). Don't let someone, especially a friend who is not an investment professional, try to convince you to take a level of risk you are not comfortable with, even if the markets are flying high and it "looks like a sure thing." Just because someone has had success investing, it doesn't make them a licensed, trained professional. Buying a medical dictionary doesn't make you a doctor—even if you put one thousand bandages on your kids' cuts and scrapes over the years. Tolerance for risk is totally personal and should be your choice. But remember, the less risk you take, the less your expectations should be for total average returns. Sorry, you cannot have your cake and eat it too—it just doesn't work that way.

Chapter 4

"I only buy no-load mutual funds because there are no fees"

When was the last time you walked into a new car dealer showroom and the salesperson said, "Go ahead, take any car you want. There is absolutely no charge for anything. We never charge our customers. Even our services and repairs are free. We are only here because we have nothing else to do today," or you go to your doctor and she says, "This one's on me. You've paid enough over the years. Besides, my parents paid for my medical education, so no worries." If that actually was to happen to you, would you be a little worried or concerned that something is just not right?

Everything has a fee somewhere—visible or hidden, it's there somewhere. I'm not saying many investments, and especially no-load funds, have high fees. Some have very low and reasonable fees. What I am saying is not to be fooled—you pay a price somewhere for everything.

There was an article written and posted on the web for *CNN Money Magazine* about mutual fund hidden costs back in the '90s. The verbiage was very short and succinct. The author disclosed *all* the fees: up-front, stated/known, and hidden for the top one hundred mutual funds at that time (load and no-load). When I read it, I was amazed at the hidden annual costs and fees. In fact, it disclosed that the average equity mutual fund at the time (and I really don't think much has changed since) has a total fee (hidden and shown) between *3–5 percent annually*! You are probably wondering, *Why are all the fees not disclosed?* and *Shouldn't that all be in the prospectus and quarterly reports?* You would think so, but for whatever reason (and candidly, I don't know the answer), it's not! Go on the web and search "hidden costs and fees on mutual funds." You will find enough information to make your head spin.

If fees are your biggest concern, that's a huge issue because "fees are only important in the absence of value." Value is determined not just by a result but by the level of service you expect and receive from whomever you are using. I used to tell clients that you pay your fees quarterly, but I earn those fees every single day.

A good financial advisor not only evaluates your needs and goals and creates a plan for you but also evaluates and suggests the correct threshold for the risk you take to achieve those goals. They also help you stay the course when things get rough and unnerving, and they will *try* to prevent you from making costly mistakes. The keyword here is *try*, because nobody can or should force your hand. The ultimate decisions are yours, and they should be a collaboration. Remember that you are paying for the advisors' skillset and experience to guide you properly. If you are going to challenge and fight with the advisor over everything or you can't trust them and constantly disagree, maybe you need someone else. You would be doing both of you a favor in the long term.

There is so much more to what you pay for than just the fee, and if this is your biggest (or only) concern, you are really missing the boat. If you were rushed to the hospital gravely ill, would you scream as you got in the Emergency Room, "Which of you doctors offer a discount!" Bottom line is, among other things, you pay for experience and even more importantly, you pay for a result.

Just prior to the height of the technology bubble (March 10, 2000) I had gotten a referral for a potential new client. During our initial meeting, we discussed many things including goals, expectations, asset management, and fees. At that time, I was using professional money managers, and I created diversity by using various managers with different investment styles (more about that in section 3). I really liked these prospective clients and hoped they would allow me to manage their finances. They didn't. He thought my fees were too high, and he was able to do the same elsewhere for much less (side note: I consider my fees to be fair and in line with firm policy and other advisors with the same experience and designations).

Approximately two years later, I got a call from this prospect asking for another meeting. He told me that his wife really liked me and was insistent that they used me regardless of fees (I knew from the first meeting that she was a very smart woman!). The reason for the change? The advisor they originally went with put their investments in almost 100 percent technology stocks because that's what was hot at the time. Asset allocation? What's that? Did the advisor have a lack of experience? Maybe. It was sad because they were retired and lost approximately half of their investment value in two years. To be totally candid (and I told them this when they transferred everything to me), if they had gone with me originally, they would have lost money too, just not nearly as much. Technology or growth stocks were down during this crisis approximately (-70 to -75 percent) and large cap value stocks were down approximately (-35 percent). This advisor had little to no diversity (the portfolio was virtually all in growth stocks), and as a result, their risk was compounded rather than reduced. Don't worry, we will discuss how to measure risk and have diversification of styles and classes in section 3.

Similarly, a personal trainer not only helps you set up a personalized weight training and nutrition program to get you into shape and/or lose weight, but their feedback and presence help keep you on track. Imagine Arnold Schwarzenegger standing over you and, in his thick Austrian accent, says, "You will do five more reps, or I'll be back" (I think you get the idea). You can just go to the gym on your own and possibly get good results, but you could get even better results, and maybe quicker, by working with a professional. Is it worth the additional expense? If you find value in doing so, then the answer would be yes.

Chapter 5

"This time it's different"

In my thirty-five years as a financial advisor, this is the quote I have heard virtually every time the stock market has had a significant decline. When you consider that the average intrayear decline is -14 percent, that would translate to at least thirty-five times during my career. But because it's been said repeatedly by many clients, it's many more times than that.

After all, every time the markets fall, it's generally for a different reason—unless we talk about politics, and I'm not going to go down that path (let's be serious, I do want to sell as many books as I can). What's interesting is, the long-term outcome is always the same—markets go down, and markets go up. Go back to what I just stated, that the average intrayear decline is -14 percent. Just like months and seasons change, cycles are a part of life. They can cryogenically freeze you when the market goes down, and if they are able to bring you back at some point in the future, the market will have gone back up, down, and back up many times since.

While I was doing a client review, and ironically the market was in the middle of one of those lovely and fun downturns I love so much, the client asked me, "When will things get back to normal?" It was a serious question, and a reasonable one too. I paused for a moment to really give thought to it and answered (honestly), "In all the years you have worked with me as your advisor, when did you think it was normal? And for that matter, what would you consider normal?" Think about it.

Of course, it seems very normal when the markets are flying high and you are making lots of money. Because, who cares, you are making money. Why challenge anything when everything is good and you are happy? In contrast, it seems not-so-normal when things go down. Why? Your gut doesn't quite have butterflies anymore when things are bad, but instead you have acid reflux? I would think the reason is because we invest to make money rather than to lose. Makes sense, and I think is very accurate. But people also get married to stay married, don't they? Unless they happen to be in Las Vegas, get very drunk, and in the morning have no idea what went on the night before. No, I'm not referring to Britney Spears's 2004 marriage to Jason Alexander that lasted all of fifty-five hours. Or if you are a baby boomer, how about Cher and Greg Allman? Their marriage lasted nine days (that's probably because Cher and Greg were older than Britany, so they must have been much wiser, right?). Thinking about this, when are celebrities lives ever normal? Maybe I need to rewrite this chapter.

As I look back on my career as a financial advisor, we definitely experienced some times that were extremely different and not normal:

- The stock market crash of 1987

- The technology bubble of 2000–2002 (the tech bubble actually ended the middle of March 2003, and 2003 ended up greater than +28 percent)
- The horrific morning of 9/11
- The financial crises of 2007–2008 (the financial crises actually ended March 9, 2009, but 2009 ended up greater than +26 percent)

However, when the cycle during those times changed direction, like every other time in history, markets went back up. An interesting fact is, when markets have steep declines (like the times described above), the time it takes for a market to go from its very bottom back to its peak is 4.2 years on average.

What if you went to your advisor July 2007 with your life savings and wanted to invest everything 100 percent in stocks (the S&P 500 index). Let's use this allocation for this example because it's the most aggressive we can be (if you were to use a more conservative allocation, know you would/should experience less volatility than the example I am about to give). You tell your advisor that you are on your way to the marina and are heading to Gilligan's Island for ten years (that's longer than the show was on TV). You will have no communication, and you will not be able to make any changes to your allocation or portfolio. Okay, let's all sing the theme song and reminisce: "No phone, no lights, no motor car, not a single luxury" Okay, maybe the cast is one hundred-plus years old or not even alive anymore, so you're not really expecting too much fun. But for this example, we are shipping you off anyway, so too bad, but enjoy it (I promise, you'll be happy with your portfolio when you return).

What if the advisor told you in no uncertain terms that for the first year and a half, you will be down approximately -50 percent. Remember, you will be stranded for ten years and can't do anything. I would assume in ten years the professors radio battery would have stopped working and Gilligan would finally start a mutiny because he was tired of the Skipper hitting him in the head with his hat for his mistakes. Sorry, I got a little carried away. Let's get back to the example. So for the first year and a half, you would be down approximately -50 percent. Would you still invest?

Here are the results: If you were afraid and did nothing and left the funds in money market, you would have earned less than 1 percent a year. By the way, inflation was about 2 percent during that period. So if you earned 1 percent and inflation was 2 percent, you would have lost about 1 percent in buying power each year. Oh, and the S&P 500, after starting off down significantly, you still would have averaged about 5 percent a year! And you got to go to Gilligan's Island!

I know this is going to sound boring, and I am repeating myself, but the solution is simple. If you are taking a level of risk you can live with in bad times, have very good diversity within the classes and styles (that's just a teaser—I will cover this in detail in section 3 so you can fully understand what real diversity is), just give it time. Time is not until you are done reading this chapter. A real market cycle is about seven to ten years. If you do that, you'll see that things aren't so different.

Chapter 6

"I need to have many advisors so I have diversity"

In some cases, I wouldn't disagree with this. Using additional advisors because they specialize in something specific like alternative investments or private equity isn't necessarily a bad thing. I'm also a believer in using an insurance specialist as well (for insurance needs, not for investments or annuities). Excluding annuities, insurance is specific for risk management and has a very important role in your portfolio outside of your investments.

Personally, I get frustrated when I see insurance people pass themselves off as financial gurus or when financial advisors pass themselves off as trained insurance people just because they hold licenses. A Certified Financial Planner® (CFP®) may be the exception to this. But the majority specialize in insurance and sell mutual funds and products similar just to round out their practice. This is opposed to having real (my opinion) investment planning and understanding the creation of true diversity in an overall portfolio. In contrast, although many financial advisors may be licensed in various types of insurance, generally that is not their specialty. I think there should be a primary investment advisor who will oversee everything and make sure the overall asset allocation is in line with your specific goals and objectives.

If you want two or three advisors because you feel like it adds to diversity, I would question your trust in any of them, which is probably why you don't want any one of them to oversee everything.

Would you use two or three CPAs so you can get varying advice? Maybe a few estate attorneys to accomplish a single task just to have a difference of opinion and stir the pot? However, you may have to use an additional attorney specific to a certain need you may have. That's actually reasonable, but your primary attorney should still oversee everything as an added set of eyes and ears to help guide you.

Much like medicine, you should have a primary care doctor, and that doctor should be involved to oversee specialists you may also be using so the primary can monitor your overall well-being.

A good advisor will (should) be happy to play the role of quarterback—not just working with specialty financial advisors but with your insurance specialist, estate attorney, CPA, and others as well. You want a team and not make it into a competition among them. If the primary advisor is not willing to do that or ridicules or downplays the others, maybe it's time for a new primary financial advisor.

I've had a few clients over the years tell me they are using multiple financial advisors, and when I suggested they have me look at everything to evaluate the overall plan, they balked and took offense (I think they anticipated I was going to try and convince them to move everything to me, which couldn't have been farther from the truth). Even after I explained my only intention is to make sure each of us are not duplicating things, which in essence would increase their risk, it obviously wasn't their plan, and they didn't want to give up control. These clients tend to make it a competition among advisors instead of treating their entire portfolio like a business. Once (maybe twice) a client doing this told me that I was underperforming their other advisor and that he was going to reevaluate everything at the end of the year. Not liking that statement, I asked, "Why are you waiting until the end of the year?" Just because I underperformed one year doesn't mean the following year the other advisor won't underperform me. An adviser should never chase performance just to look good.

Much like using a mix of investment styles such as large cap, mid cap, small cap (growth and value for each) and international investments (this is what Modern Portfolio Theory is, and we will talk extensively about that in section 3), they are *not* supposed to all move together in lock-step. There should be negative correlation (moving in varying directions) between each style to help reduce overall risk.

Think of a baseball team. All nine players do not play the same position, and everyone doesn't run together to where the ball is after it's hit. They all have their respective positions and their own jobs to perform. Same with batters. Generally, batters 1 and 2 are not homerun (longball) hitters. Their job is to just get on base so batters 3, 4, and 5 can bring them home and score runs. Batters 6,7, and 8 fill the gap. Why does the pitcher bat last? It's not because they can't get a hit, but it's because the team manager doesn't want them to swing hard and hurt their arm. They need them to pitch and prevent the other team from getting hits and scoring. Why is there only one manager or head coach? While there can be assistants for specific areas, the head coach oversees everything and makes the calls. Investing is no different.

Here's the bottom line:

Diversity is what you should strive for when investing (not just to get performance, but reduce risk too). A good advisor will provide proper diversity, which will reduce your risk while you move toward your goals. Making it a competition between advisors (unless you are using specialists like I explained) is counterproductive at the very least. Hire quality people and look for quality results, even if you have to pay more. Build a team of professionals who are willing to work as one rather than have arm-wrestling matches every month to see who is better.

If you challenge an advisor to outperform your other advisor(s), they may take risk they normally wouldn't for fear of losing the client, and in the end, it will hurt you. Personally, I wouldn't take on a client who would put me in such a position, not because I'm better and it's beneath me but because it would put the client in harm's way for improper diversification.

Chapter 7

"I know I am in a low tax bracket, but I don't want to pay taxes. I would rather make 2 percent tax-free than 7 percent that's taxable"

This is also not an unusual thought process for many because, who really wants to pay taxes? So I viewed this comment as just reactionary opposed to a thought-out bottom-line result.

This particular client was semiretired and had very little income (she worked part-time), so every dollar earned in investment income was important.

In a nutshell, it's what you keep in the end that matters (after taxes). It's much better to earn 10 percent and pay tax than earn 0. I know that statement may seem foolish, because it is, but I needed to make a strong point. Now that I have your attention, let's make it more realistic. If you earn 5 percent on a CD (that's taxable) and your total tax, federal and state combined, is 35 percent (I just made that up, so don't hold me to it and ask your tax advisor what your total tax bracket is for a real number), you would net after tax 3.25 percent. Simple math: 5 percent taxable return minus 35 percent for taxes equals 3.25 percent net. Let's not complicate it any more than we need to. So if you have a choice of 5percent taxable or anything less than 3.25percent tax-free and you are in a 35 percent total tax bracket, go with the higher after-tax number (obviously, adjust the number to your actual tax bracket to see a real comparison). That's also assuming both investments are of the same quality. If one is of lesser quality, I generally lean toward the higher quality investment because you should be investing, not speculating.

I remember hearing as a kid that you are much better off earning less in income because when you earn more, you will be in a higher tax bracket. That's only partially true. As of this writing, we do not pay flat taxes. So only a portion of your income will pay a higher rate, not all of it. So the more you earn, the more you take home after taxes. That's the same as saying, "I don't want to win the lottery because I will have to pay tax!" If you really feel that way, I am very happy to take your winning lottery ticket and pay the taxes.

It's all about what you keep after taxes that matters. It really is as simple as that, so I'm not going to stretch this chapter out any more than it needs to be.

Chapter 8

"Why am I paying capital gains taxes? I don't want to pay taxes. This is terrible"

I leased my first Mercedes-Benz in 1989. When I took it in for the annual required service, I was quite impressed with the size and cleanliness of the waiting area and having a variety of bagels, cream cheese, pastries, and coffee for customers to enjoy. Although routine, this service was major in the time it would take to complete, so they gave me a loaner car and said they will call me when the car is ready, probably the following day. They couldn't have been nicer, and the service was impeccable. They even washed my car! Just what you would expect from Mercedes-Benz.

When I picked up my car the following day, I had to write a check for $1,200. That was the cost of this routine maintenance. The next day, a representative from the dealership called me to ask if I was satisfied with everything and asked for my feedback. For a brief moment, I pondered how to answer. After all, I brought in a car that was running great and in perfect condition. I had no issues whatsoever with the vehicle prior to bringing it in, and I was only there for routine service that was required. I told the rep that the service and their staff were really fantastic and that having breakfast for the customers was quite a treat (I never got fed at other dealerships). Given a clean, new loaner car to use while my car was being serviced made the experience that much better. But in all fairness, I brought in a car that worked perfectly and got back a car that looked and drove the same as when I brought it in. However, my bank account had $1,200 less than when I started. It's hard to be singing songs of happiness or wanting to do this often when I really didn't see a difference. Granted, the bagels were quite good (most would agree that there is nothing like a fresh New York bagel), but I never paid $1,200 for a bagel with a schmear and a carwash before (maybe that would be an interesting business to open: have your car washed and get a bagel on us for only $1,200).

My point of telling this story is that it's much like paying taxes. Sometimes it's difficult to find value for what you just paid. Like being able to finally afford a new Mercedes, if you are paying taxes (and hopefully lots of taxes), you are doing something very right. It means you have made money.

Based on the realized capital gains in the taxable portion of your portfolio, you will have taxes due (qualified retirement plans, such as IRAs, grow tax-deferred, and until you take a distribution, there shouldn't be any tax liability), which brings me to realized and unrealized capital gains.

You only pay taxes on gains that are realized. Let me explain what that means: if you purchase a stock for fifty dollars. and it goes up in value to one hundred dollars but do not sell it, there are no taxes due at that time (gains or losses occur during a calendar year, January 1 to December 31). That's because the gain is not realized until it is sold. Whatever calendar year, the stock is actually sold when you will either pay tax on the gain or take a loss if it's less than what you paid for it. If the stock was held more than twelve months, it is also considered a long-term gain, and generally the tax is less than for a short-term gain (held less than one year). Allow me to provide you with a quick disclaimer: I am not a qualified tax person or CPA, so any tax-related issues should always be discussed with a tax professional.

Here's where it can get a little odd and confusing. I've had many years where clients called me upset because I told them we had a good year but they had losses. How can that be? (I really loved those calls.) That's because their portfolio went up in value, but nothing in the portfolio was sold to create a capital gain. Hence, that is an unrealized gain, because to have a gain, you must have a buy *and* a sell to complete the cycle. If securities were sold during the year at a loss and the value of the overall portfolio was up for the year, they have appreciation in value but will actually take a loss on their tax return. (Feel free to read that a few times, as many have a difficult time understanding. Remember, you don't do this for a living and are only human, so cut yourself some slack.) In contrast, and these are the calls I really disliked, you could have a loss for the year (where the portfolio started January 1 higher than where it finished December 31) and still have a realized capital gain because of securities sold during the year at a profit. This is why it is important to use professionals not just to handle things for you but they should also explain intricate things so you understand and make informed decisions.

The bottom line is, paying taxes is a good thing. The more tax you pay on your income, the more you earned. The more you pay in real estate tax, the more your home is worth (hopefully, with a very little or no mortgage). The more you pay in capital gains, the more your portfolio made in profit.

Chapter 9

"I need a favor... I need to make a quick $25,000"

This was the inspiration for the title of this book, and you are about to see why.

Rather than just provide you with a logical answer to the question, I want to provide the transcript from the call so you can feel the entire experience (it may not be the exact transcript, but it's very close). Yes, I actually answered it this way, and yes, you can say I was a bit of a moron for doing this. But I couldn't refuse the opportunity to make a point. And I've known this client for a long time, and he knows I am a bit (okay, quite a bit) of a jackass at times when it comes to getting my points across.

I know this quote may seem absurd or made up, but this has been asked of me quite a few times, all with slight variations. Admit it, you have thought of asking your financial advisor the same thing but felt embarrassed and passed on asking. I'm proud of you! Well, here it is:

Client: Can I ask you a favor?

Me: Sure, what do you need?

Client: I need to make a quick $25,000. What can we do?

(A very long pause)

Me: I wished you called me a few days ago.

Client: Why?

Me: We are not allowed to solicit this to any clients or even tell them about this unless they ask us first, so please never mention this to anyone. But every year, we are allowed to give a client a quick $25,000 if they ask. It has to be completely unsolicited. Ironically, a few days ago, another client called me and had the same request. So I told them about this one-time offer and just put the $25,000 in their account. They didn't have to do anything more. I just gave them the money they needed.

Client: Seriously? OMG, I wished I called you last week. I didn't know you can do that. That's awesome!

At this point, I really thought about calling the book *Are You %$#@*#% Kidding Me?*, but I didn't think anyone would publish it.

Even Bernie Madoff didn't offer a deal like that! Anything that sounds too good to be true usually is. No way, period. There are no *"get rich quick"* methods, and if someone offers one to you, run, because it's probably not legal and you most likely will lose your money.

I'm amazed by ads I see on TV or in magazines to make significant money in stocks, options, precious metals, commodities, whatever. What's worse is how many fall victim to it and lose their hard-earned money to con artists who should be jailed or stoned. (No, I'm not saying we should send them to Colorado!)

Scamming happens to the best of us, and once again, I will use myself as the example. Only this time, I was young and stupid. (I know you are probably thinking that now I am older and stupid, but that's not nice!) It happened when I was in college in New York City and walking down Eight or Ninth Avenue with a friend while on a break from class. Someone approached us and asked if we were interested in buying a gold watch. He said he needed the money and he was willing to give it away for twenty dollars. My friend jumped at the opportunity. Then I jumped all over my friend saying, "How could you be so stupid—twenty dollars for a gold watch. Are you kidding? (I apparently use that phrase a lot.) You know you just got robbed!" I couldn't believe he bought the watch. Keep in mind that at that time, neither of us had any money growing up in Levittown, and twenty dollars was my weekly train ticket for the Long Island railroad. But as we got about one hundred yards away, I started thinking to myself, *What if the watch is real and the guy who sold it really needed quick money—would I feel like an idiot if I passed up a gold watch for twenty dollars?* Well, (I admit, stupidly) I turned around and went back to the guy selling the watches and asked if he has another. Another? He probably had fifty of them in his trench coat (this could have been right out of a *Seinfeld* or *Curb Your Enthusiasm* episode). Not wanting to pass up such a great deal, I bought one too! In less than four hours, both of our wrists were turning green from the coating and the gold started to peel off! It *was* too good to be true.

If you need to make a quick $25,000 or more, do it the old-fashioned way—work overtime, lots of overtime. Or take ten dollars to twenty dollars and buy some scratch-off lottery tickets. At least you know the money will go to the state for higher education

Chapter 10

"Let's get out of the market. We can get back in *after* it gets back on track"

This may sound like a simple process that's easy to execute, but in reality, it almost would never happen. Once your emotions take over, you are driven more by fear than success.

Let's discuss down periods because those are the times you need to get through to stay for the good times. Since 1980, the average intrayear decline is (-14%); yes, that is normal and needs to be accepted to move forward. Yet only approximately 20 percent of the time has the S&P 500 finished down for the year. Go one step further to note that the average time it takes to go from a decline bottom back to the peak is approximately 4.20 years.

But when things look like the world is about to end, it's incredibly difficult to imagine that a reversal is on horizon and not far off, so panic takes over. And many investors run for the nearest door and take their losses. Many would say they want to wait until things calm down and will get back in. But by the time the markets have shown stability and are back on the mend, a good part of the return has already occurred, and it's too late. At this time, it's worth taking a minute and going back to the "Cycle of Emotions" chart in section 1.

We are all human and react to our emotions. To that point, I will use myself in this example. Because even as a financial advisor for many years, I still feel the same emotions as everyone else and bleed when I'm cut. Most times, I know what is the right thing to do and I act accordingly (based upon statistics and market history), but sometimes, it's just too much for anyone, me included. By early March 2009, the United States was at the height of the worst financial crises since the Great Depression. We were literally steps from falling into the abyss and going into another Depression (literally). From October 9, 2007, to March 9, 2009, the S&P 500 Index was (-56 percent) with no end to the decline in sight. It was the worst I have ever seen in my career (and life). At the time (I wasn't thinking about retiring then), I was virtually 100 percent in equities and had no problem accepting that level of risk for my family because I had very good diversity (I am a long-term investor). My business model was fee-based, not commission-based upon my assets and asset growth or decline. That meant that not only was my portfolio down significantly but so was my income. So if I am going to be completely candid, I will tell you honestly I was scared about what was happening to our country and economy.

The last thing on my mind March 9, 2009, (the very bottom of the crises) was adding any cash I had to my portfolio or even remotely suggesting that to my clients. I have always prided myself on doing the same for me as I do for my clients (I am not a fan of conflicts of interest). But let's say you waited a month or four months, be honest (I was), when would you have gotten back in? After that crises, most didn't get back in the market for years and some still have not and never will. Here is some real performance for the S&P 500 in the months that followed March 9, 2009:

- March 9, 2009 (676.53)–April 1, 2009 (848.15) = +25.37% for less than one month
- March 9, 2009 (676.53)–August 1, 2009 (1009.73) = +49.25% for less than six months
- March 9, 2009 (676.53)–January 1, 2010 (1123.58) = +66.08% for less than ten months

Do you think it would have been better to stay the course (again if you have the right allocation and are diversified well)? I did with my own funds, and virtually all my clients did too. We may have a little extra gray hair and wrinkles as a result, but because we didn't lose as much money as we could have, there is ample money for hair color and Botox!

Here is an analogy that I have used and made sense (at least to me): 'why the day after Thanksgiving do people get up in the middle of the night, brave the harsh Winter weather (especially in very cold climates), go to their local shopping mall to stand on line for hours, and trample those in front of them when the doors open to save a few dollars on merchandise they probably don't even need, but when it comes to investing in the stock market, they will gleefully buy when prices for stocks are at all-time highs? Can you imagine going into a store to make a purchase and insist on paying the highest price the merchandise was ever at and make them add an additional 20 percent to make you feel it's worth it? So why do investors run for the doors when the markets are down and buy like crazy when the market is high? Do you really have to wonder why so many never make money in their investments and, to make matters worse, make the same mistake over and over? Their answer, "This time it's different!" Sorry to disagree, but I don't think so.

Chapter 11

"What's the average return for the stock market historically, around 20 percent, right?"

This comment comes up much more than you would think, and perception can create reality in your mind. This is more off base than you would imagine, especially since 2000.

I had gotten a referral from a client, a retired couple who had a few different advisors prior to meeting with me. They said they were not happy with the advisors they had presently and with those they have used in the past. They added that they were tired of losing money every year and really do not want to take much risk either, as the assets they showed me needed to last through the remainder of their lives. Seemed like a fair request, at least until I asked them what they thought would be a reasonable expected average return over the next ten years or so. That's when I uncovered the reason why they constantly lost money in their investments.

The husband very calmly (and matter-of-factly) stated, "We'll take 10–12 percent a year." I encourage you to reread his response and ask yourself if that's reasonable. By the way, the keyword in what he stated was *take*—they are willing to *take* 10–12 percent a year and with very little risk. Allow me to demonstrate "take" in my opinion. "I would really love to win the lottery jackpot for $10 million dollars, but I'll *take* $1 million dollars." *Take* is a term of acceptance—"*if I have to,*" "not really what I was hoping for, but *I'll take it*, and it would be okay."

My next question was if they knew what the historic returns of the stock market and also what the average return has been from 2000–2009 where we experienced two different (-50%) declines, the technology bubble from March 2000–March 2002, and the financial crises from July 2007–March 2009? They looked stumped and puzzled, just like I do with almost every question when I watch *Jeopardy!*

I didn't want to be condescending, so I said, "No worries, let me give you the answers so we can be on the same page." Here are those numbers:

- Historically, the compounded return of the S&P 500 is 10 percent annually
- Historically, the simple interest return of the S&P 500 is 12 percent annually
- However, from 2009–2018 average for the S&P 500 is approximately 5 percent annually (because of the two (-50%) declines during that period

Keep in mind that these numbers mean you would have been invested 100 percent in equities or stocks, not exactly low risk.

In my opinion, based on what they told me, I suggested an allocation of no more than 65 percent equity and 35 percent fixed income (maybe even fifty-fifty?). I also stated that their expected return should be somewhere between 5–7 percent annually over a ten-year cycle after fees (and let's not confuse this with a guaranteed return because there is risk in investing, and there are no guarantees). They said they wouldn't have it and said they need 10–12 percent a year. Now they were not willing to *take* 10–12 percent a year, but they were *demanding* it.

After my next comment, I knew we weren't going to be best friends and sing kumbaya together. I said (very nicely) that I really don't think their present or past advisors really intended for them to lose money during down periods. They created allocations to meet their expectations, which in my opinion were still too risky. I think those advisors should have told that to them during the interview process rather than hoping for a good market (invest based on statistics, not hope and prayers). I added that personally I would rather see them walk away because I will not expose them to the level of risk needed to accomplish the returns they are expecting because they will only be unhappy and leave me, too, on the next downturn. I'd rather a client accepts reasonable expectations from the beginning. Needless to say, they left my office in search of an advisor willing to try to help them.

It's important to understand historic returns for stocks and bonds. It's just as important to look at where the economy is presently (earnings on public companies, consumer spending, current interest rates at various maturities, and what direction interest rates are heading, up or down?). Also, give thought to how much downside you can accept during a bad quarter or year. Be honest with yourself. Remember, you cannot achieve upside without accepting down periods. You have to stay through the bad times in order to get to the good times.

This will help you have reasonable expectations for your portfolio return and allow you to manage risk by creating a suitable allocation between stocks, bonds, and cash.

Chapter 12

"I don't care if I lost much less than what the market went down—I still lost money"

You cannot expect to make profits when markets decline. Maybe once in a while that will happen because when markets decline, not everything goes down. But generally, if you walk outside during a monsoon, you should expect to get wet. You can prepare for it by having a good allocation and style diversity (like wearing a raincoat and having an umbrella), but your portfolio will/should go down. It's simple logic. You can skip to chapter 16 where I discuss my thoughts when clients have stated that they "know an advisor who has never lost money for their clients," but I would rather you read the rest of this chapter first. You already bought the book, so why not get the most out of it?

Losing less than the benchmark you are comparing to is where you should find great value with whomever you are working with. Downside capture (the amount you go down versus whatever benchmark you compare to) is so much more important than upside capture (the amount you go up versus whatever benchmark you compare to). If you are comparing to the S&P 500, (assuming you would be 100% in stocks,) and that index declines (-10%), but you *only* go down (-9%), you are actually doing well by mathematical measure. Yes, I use the word *only* and you are still down (-9%) which is awful, but you are outperforming the benchmark. If you are down (-8%) you are doing even better, and (-7%) better still, and so on. Obviously, if your allocation is 65% equity and 35% fixed income, the benchmark you should be comparing to would be comprised of a like allocation: 65% S&P 500 and 35% bond index (adjust the equity portion if you have any percent in international exposure by adding that percentage amount to an international index).

Face it, nobody wants to lose money. If you invest in anything—a home, business, whatever—and always think you will make money, you weren't taught very well. You are not entitled. If you fall off a bicycle, expect to scrape your knee, get bruised, or maybe worse.

As an advisor, this was always a tough conversation because many clients just don't want to hear it or accept that they can lose money. For my own investments, I would much rather lose less during down periods (preservation) and make less during up periods (participation). Like an old golf saying, "You drive for show, but putt for dough." Wouldn't you much rather drive the ball down the center of the fairway all the time, maybe not as long as your friends, but never be in the rough or in trouble and sink every putt to win all their money? They may brag about how far they can hit the ball off the tee, but you'll have their cash in your pocket to go out for dinner that night.

You will see a common thread throughout this book. It will always come down to risk and how much you are willing to take (or should take) to feel comfortable during downturns. That will dictate the correct asset allocation you should have between stocks, bonds, and cash. If you cannot emotionally handle down periods, chances are, you are taking too much risk. You don't adjust your risk (allocation to stocks, bonds, and cash) because the market is good or bad. Rather, you adjust the holdings within the portfolio (styles within the classes) to adjust to the market.

Risk is who you are as an individual at a certain point in your lifetime. What I mean is, regardless of how conservative or aggressive you are as a person, as you age and/or experience life events, your level of risk should decline. This may be because you don't have the earning years left to make losses back, or based on your lifestyle and the assets you already have, you don't want to have to go back to work. But you have to accept downside if you want upside—just less downside, hopefully. And that's a good thing.

Chapter 13

"I realize the market went down, and I still made a positive return. I need more"

We all would like more, right? Who wouldn't want more? But let's be realistic. If the market is down and you make a positive return, you should not only be happy, you should be ecstatic (we are only talking about the stock portion of your portfolio). Like running a business, the financial markets move in cycles. Some years are up very big, some years up not so big, some years flat, and some years down (oh yeah, and some years can also be down quite a bit). Just like a business, when the economy is slow, you want to keep your head above water so you can be there for the good times. You should also expect some years your portfolio will have a loss, but hopefully a small loss. But this client statement was "Even though the market went down and I was up slightly, I need more." Read that statement again—even though the market was down slightly, they actually had a positive return for the year. I'm sorry, you may have been spoiled as a child, had a privileged life, and maybe even received trophies in sports you participated in just for showing up and not actually winning, but that's not real life. You can need everything. You just may not be able to get it. There is no entitlement here.

You may want to go back a chapter (chapter 12), where I discussed that going down less than your comparison benchmark is actually quite good.

My goal in managing money for clients and myself was always to do better during down markets (lose less), even if I made less during up markets. If I was fortunate to be up, even slightly, during a downturn, I was very happy. I just wouldn't expect to outperform the markets significantly every year. It's not reasonable. There will also be many years you will underperform your benchmark. When that happens ask your advisor for the reasons why. If your advisor took a more cautious approach because of geopolitical issues or other valid reasons to protect you, it's unfair to change advisors. Nobody is perfect. If you know your advisor is ethical, has integrity, and puts your needs first, you would be making a huge mistake to chastise or fire them because of poor performance for one or two years.

You absolutely have the right to want more, but you just shouldn't always expect it. If you do, you are setting yourself up for disappointment. However, let's not confuse portfolio performance with client service. This is entirely different. A high level of client service is something you should always expect and receive, regardless of what the markets are doing. That's a big part of your fees and what you are paying for. For that, my expectations will always be high, and I wouldn't settle for less.

Chapter 14

"Why does my portfolio seem to go down as much as the market, but when the market is up, I don't go up nearly as much?"

Sometimes, there is just no explanation, and your portfolio will move independent of the markets. But there could be a couple of reasons that it may seem like you are getting the short end of the stick.

When markets go up, especially by quite a bit, most don't notice (or even care) because you are making money. However, when markets decline, emotions step in, and we don't always see things rationally or correctly. Instead, we interpret or see what we want to see. Many times, I have heard clients talk about their losses in dollars rather than in percentage. Looking at it this way is just not right. Why? Because the market doesn't move in dollars. You never hear it reported on the evening news, "Today the financial markets went down quite a bit, and you probably lost $20,000." What the news anchor would state is, "Today the financial markets declined about (-1 percent)."

If you have $100,000 invested and your portfolio goes down $1000, it's exactly the same as investing $1,000,000 and losing $10,000. Both are the same -1 percent decline. Using percentage as your metric for performance is a constant, regardless of how much money you have invested. I wouldn't disagree that losing $10,000 is more painful than losing $1,000, but wouldn't you rather have $1,000,000 in investments instead of $100,000? I know that sounds foolish, but it's all relative. Using percentage is the only way to be fair and consistent in your evaluation.

The other reason is a little more complicated. What is "the market" anyway? Are you looking at the Dow Jones Average (DJIA), which is made up of only thirty stocks, or are you using the S&P 500, which is made up of five hundred stocks, or the NASDAQ market (over the counter stocks), which is comprised of over 3,300 company listings? If you are using the New York Stock Exchange (NYSE), there are approximately 2,800 stocks/companies listed. The majority of investors look at all three of these indexes.

What if the S&P 500 is down (-2 percent) for the day and, on the NYSE, there are 2,700 stocks down and a hundred are up (not everything moves together, and many companies move independent of the averages)? Luckily, the fifty stocks you own are all up. Or the market is +2% for the day with 2,600 stocks up and 100 down. Unfortunately, your holdings are among the down stocks. There's a paradigm shift to think about.

Is your portfolio 100 percent in stocks? If you have some of your investments in bonds (fixed income), is it fair to compare your performance to an index that is 100 percent equities? Let's go one step further: what if all (or a good portion) of your stock allocation is invested using a growth style and value is in favor? The point is, there are many ways to look at this, and there is no one right way. Markets are complicated and it's important to understand what markets are made up of—growth, value, large cap, mid cap, small cap, international, emerging markets, and many more. Don't worry, in chapter 33, I discuss equity styles and classes in great detail and in simple terms so you will understand it. I promise not to complicate it more than it is.

Let's be honest. There are times that you can't make heads or tails of the situation, and there really isn't a good explanation. Fabricating an explanation just for the sake of having one is not right. If your portfolio underperforms your benchmark every so often, I wouldn't get overly concerned. When you review your portfolio with your advisor, ask her thoughts on why she thinks it occurs. If it happens very often, maybe there was a momentum style shift, and changes need to be made. That would call for a serious conversation with your advisor because maybe you are not diversified properly. Before you make the call, go back and look at your portfolio over many months and do a comparison to the appropriate market index (or blended index including fixed income if you are not 100 percent in stocks). Make sure you are consistent in which index or blended index you are comparing to. You can always find an index (or indexes) you either outperformed or underperformed on any given day, week, month, quarter, or year. It's important to know what you will compare to at the onset of creating your asset allocation so there are no questions later. Always use percentages and not dollars to gauge performance so you can make a consistent, clear, and justifiable evaluation.

Chapter 15

"When will the volatility end? What does your firm say? I need a date when things will start moving back up"

This is the perfect example of behavioral finance (see chapter 1). If you are really honest with yourself, you probably felt and thought exactly the same at one time or another. My goal for writing this book was not to make fun of anyone because they had the courage to verbalize their thoughts and fears while investing when things got rough and chaotic. It was to shed light that we are all human and have similar feelings, no matter how bizarre these questions may seem. It's to help people realize that emotions and irrational behavior take control of our thoughts and actions when investing and to offer solutions on how to deal with them better so you don't make mistakes that can ultimately cost you dearly.

This client was panicky because of geopolitical chaos adding to a significant but not unusual market decline, so emotions were running very high. When the client demanded to know what exact date my firm was saying the markets would turn around and go back up, I was brutally honest. I said that if any financial advisor or company gave an exact date as to when markets would rise and fall, I would run fast, because they would be lying. I tried to offer market history and statistics (math usually doesn't lie, and history is a good gauge in the financial markets to determine future behavior, although never a guarantee), but the client wouldn't have any of it and hung up. I stand by my actions of telling the client the facts and truth, even though that was not what he wanted to hear. I was always (well, mostly) respectful, but I never wanted to patronize a client. I felt they deserved more, and nothing is better than honesty.

It's very important to note that the average intrayear decline for the S&P 500 is approximately (-14 percent), and that is normal and should be expected. It's just as important to note that historically after these significant declines, the markets rebound swiftly and have finished down (for the same year) approximately only 20 percent of the time. That means even after steep declines, the market has had positive returns 80 percent of the time. To put this in perspective, if a batter in baseball gets a hit one out of every three times at bat, they become a Hall of Famer (aside from making gazillions of dollars). Thank goodness surgeons don't use the same metric as baseball play-ers to determine how good they are!

Investing is *not* gambling. Buying quality stocks is buying into America's economy and should be treated as long-term ventures. Every day is not sunny. Financial markets, like weather and all busi-nesses, are cyclical. They don't move in a linear way, meaning straight up or down.

Think of it this way: If you had a million dollars to buy a McDonald's franchise (assuming you can get one), you would be putting your money into a single location. Granted, you don't see many go out of business, but that is also not a guarantee of success either. If you took the same million dollars and bought the stock, you would be buying into the entire company along with full management to run it. Aside from potential growth, you would also get a dividend quarterly. Let me be very clear that I am *not* recommending that you should buy McDonald's or anything else. This book doesn't offer any advice—actually, it's quite the opposite. It's to help you avoid mistakes and tell you what *not* to do.

My point is, this too is a long-term investment, and you cannot expect to make money every day, week, month, or even year. You should expect and anticipate there will be times your investments can and will lose money. However, the loss or gain will only be realized if you sell. So what's the solution? Simple. Don't panic, and treat your portfolio the same way you would treat any business you would own. Also, try not to hang up on your financial adviser when they are giving you honest advice. Most of us are very sensitive.

Chapter 16

"I know an advisor who has never lost money for their clients"

I think in this day and age, we all know at least one money manager who comes to mind: Bernie Madoff (feel free to add your own thoughts once you read his name). Unfortunately, I am sure there are many more just like him that haven't been caught yet.

Years back, I played golf with a few very successful guys who used Madoff to manage their money. I also knew others who had their money with him too. I had heard the Madoff name many times before his arrest and conviction but never really heard anything bad at the time. When these people talked about Madoff and how good he was, I just listened and never really said much. I made a habit of never badmouthing another advisor because, in essence, I would be insulting the person who hired them. If someone made a choice to use someone or a specific firm, it was *their* choice.

I also tried not to mix business with pleasure, unless they approached me for advice and help. We have all gotten those calls from friends we haven't spoken with in twenty-plus years. After a couple of hours on the phone reminiscing about old times, they hit you with a "by the way" and the sales pitch is front and center. It's not long when you realized why they really called. At that point, I quickly remember why I haven't spoken to them for many years.

I'm a big believer that when something is too good to be true, it usually is. How can anyone always have a good year? Nobody is that good. It's like the neighbor who is always cheery and never seems to have a bad day. Then one day he goes crazy. When they interview many of his neighbors on the news that evening, they say, "He was a quiet guy, always so nice." It's always the quiet ones to be wary of.

Most importantly, never chase performance. Performance is not retroactive. If you feel very confident, first evaluate what style of management they use (growth, value, sector rotation, etc. We will cover this in detail in section 3). If they can't answer that, maybe they aren't a good choice. If they do answer it, ask to see how their comparable benchmark did during the same time frame. If they are "always up significantly" above their benchmark or up when their benchmark is down, be skeptic. It's okay to ask for more information before you give them money to manage. It also has to make sense to you. If they don't already, ask them to simplify their answers so you fully understand.

Wayne Gretzky, one of the best all-time hockey players, was quoted as saying, "A good hockey player plays where the puck is. A great hockey player plays where the puck is going to be. I skate to where the puck is going to be, not where it has been."

Look forward, not behind. If it's too good to be true, it usually is, and there's more to it.

Chapter 17

"My son is doing a much better job than you are"

When the client first told me this, I was quite impressed. After all, I have three kids that I adore. After all, what's better than being proud of your children?

We all know many young adults who are extremely bright and have a good understanding of the financial markets. Kids today are computer literate by the time they start kindergarten. When I was in kindergarten, school was only half a day, and aside from naptime and playtime, they taught us how to write our name. What's even funnier, we had the whole school year just to learn to write our name.

I asked the client to share the portfolio not to pick it apart but to applaud his child for an outstanding job. And selfishly, I really wanted to know what he was buying that was doing so well and what research he was using to help him with his decisions.

When I asked the client to show me the statement listing all the securities, he said he didn't have to because he knew the holdings, or should I say holding. Yes, only one security, and to make it worse, it was a penny stock. One security is not a portfolio. Being proud of your children is one thing, but comparing a single security to a well-diversified portfolio is not a comparison.

Chapter 18

"I am going to retire in a couple of years. When should we get out of the market?"

I hate to be blunt, but you should get out of the market and stop investing when you stop breathing. Even then, your heirs will take their inheritance, and they should continue to invest. What should change at different points in your lifetime is your allocation and risk. As your life evolves from the capital accumulation stage to a capital preservation stage, your allocation should adjust as well.

Warning: You should never increase your risk to a point that it could threaten your net worth for the sole purpose of hoping to earn more.

If you are retired, the feeling and expectation that you must always have a positive return is not unusual, but unrealistic. Changing your entire portfolio to CDs, US Treasuries, muni bonds, and other fixed income vehicles is not the answer. You still need to outpace inflation, especially in the early years of retirement while you are younger and you have to look at life expectancy so you don't outlive your money. The only asset class that has consistently outpaced inflation over the long term is stocks.

First, look at the current risk you are taking and your allocation (almost everything I talk about in this book will come down to the risk you take, or should take, and your expectations for an average return over a long-term period). Once you retire, capital preservation is going to be your primary goal, and keeping pace with inflation will be second. Your first step is to do a very in-depth cash flow analysis. No, not the typical cash flow statement most create that is minimal and only includes your car payments, electric, mortgage, taxes, and basic items. You have to be very thorough and include everything from gifts (especially if you have grandchildren), spending money, taxes, supplemental healthcare payments, clothing, travel, dry cleaning, haircuts, pocket money, etc. Be honest and try not to leave anything out. If you overestimate, that's okay. Because if you don't spend that much, you'll have money left over, as opposed to not listing everything and coming up short at the end of the year. I can tell you that if you are completely honest and don't leave anything out, you will be somewhat depressed after you do this and may not want to retire so fast. But don't fret, because in section 3, we will discuss guidelines to use for cash flow distribution amounts to avoid running out of money in retirement. Don't give up yet and keep pushing forward until the end of the book.

First, let's go back to risk and what it really means. There is always risk, even if you are invested 100 percent in short-term US Treasuries. I'm sure you've heard the phrase "If I just left it under the mattress, I would have done better." There definitely are years that phrase would be hard to argue with. If you do not invest and just stay in cash, you are guaranteed to lose money in other ways. Not investing will result in a 0 percent return, and *you will lose to inflation*. That's known as nonmarket risk. It's true. Not investing also carries a risk factor most never think about (or choose not to think about). If you want to challenge my statement, look at what it cost ten, twenty, or thirty years ago for a car, a gallon of gasoline, or to feed your family and compare it to the cost today. Inflation is very real. I remember when I graduated college, I aspired to earn $250 a week because then I would be swimming in money. Maybe back then, being single and still living at home with my parents, that may have been true. For many, that amount wouldn't cover their monthly overhead today. By the way, $250 a week translates to about $13,000 a year. In today's dollars, that's poverty.

Back in 1969, Ford sold a car named Maverick for $1,995. Granted you had to choose a very ugly blue or bright-orange color and the seats were an awful plaid, but the base price was only $1,995! To replace the four tires on my car today costs more than that. Just to replace a key fob costs about $350.

If you are a baby boomer, you may remember gasoline at fifty cents a gallon, and someone actually pumped the gas and checked your oil, which for some strange reason was always a half a quart short. Hmm, automobiles have come a long way since the sixties and seventies. When I was fourteen, I worked in a pizzeria, and a slice of pizza and a small drink was fifty cents (not to be confused with the rapper 50 Cent). What about going to the movies for only a dollar, and when you went to the candy counter, they didn't have to offer you a payment plan to buy a soda and popcorn?

Inflation is very real, and the only way to outpace it is by investing. Don't be so quick to sell all your investments. Instead, finish reading this book and create a well–thought out strategy you can be comfortable with so you can enjoy your retirement. After all the years of hard work you put in, you deserve it!

Chapter 19

"I need money for cash flow, but the market is down. Should we wait a week or two until the market goes back up to take the money?"

It's always best not to time markets. It's also a good idea to create a cash flow plan for withdrawals from your investments so you are not in a situation where you are always worried about the current market conditions.

If you need to take small amounts from your portfolio periodically (let's say $10,000, $20,000, or $30,000), mathematically it doesn't make sense to wait and see how the market performs to "hopefully" get a "little" extra return.

Let me give you an example. You need a one-time distribution of $20,000, and for the past month or so, the S&P 500 has been down. It also looks like it's poised for a rebound. Remember, there are never guarantees as to when the financial markets will go up or down, regardless of what the "clowns" (financial guru of the month) say on television. If you decided to wait and see what happens in the market (now you are market timing, which historically does not work), and the markets miraculously rose +10 percent in the next month, it would add only $2,000 to your portfolio (10 percent on the $20,000 you would have taken). Before you get excited about a +10 percent monthly return, look up the historic monthly moves in the S&P 500 to see how many times it's actually happened. Probably a handful of times since the 1920s. Typical market moves are generally +/-1 percent daily.

Even a market increase of +5 percent in any given month is outstanding and not very common. So if you decided to wait a month or so before you took that $20,000 distribution and the market rose +5 percent, it would only translate to an additional $1,000. Is it really worth the risk to wait for a possible $1,000 additional when you need the money anyway? I don't think so. Look at the bigger picture for clarity. Chances are, if you are taking a periodic distribution of $20,000, your portfolio is probably greater than $1,000,000 (see chapter 22 about suggested annual distributions so you don't run out of money). Is it worth taking the risk and waiting for hopefully $1,000 on a million-dollar-plus portfolio?

To avoid taking money as needed, it's best to create a proper cash flow statement to see what your annual needs will be. In chapter 36, I discuss creating a proper cash flow statement that will include everything (not just the basics). Still, you will encounter times when additional funds are needed, so thinking clearly and not trying to time markets as to when to take the funds is important.

Chapter 20

"Why would I buy the NASDAQ Index now when it's down so much from its high?"

People love sales. They will stand in line for hours exhausted in the freezing rain or snow the day after Thanksgiving at 2:00 AM to be first in line when the stores open for the day after Thanksgiving sales events. They will buy Groupons and look through the Sunday newspaper and clip coupons for the biggest bargains, yet when the financial markets have pullbacks, they run for the doors to get out as fast as they can. Typically, weeks or months later, they have regrets and wish they stayed and didn't react. Unfortunately for many, they repeat the process during the next pullback.

As a result of the dot.com bubble, by the first quarter of 2003, the NASDAQ had declined from its high in early 2000 approximately (-75%). I was suggesting to a relatively new client that we put some of her investments in NASDAQ companies (growth). Although we had many conversations prior about asset allocation, she was upset that I would suggest investing in the NASDAQ after such a steep decline. Actually, she wasn't just upset I was suggesting this, she was downright against it. Even after I explained that the time to add funds to a style is when it's been beaten down and the style looks as though it's coming back into favor, she argued and refused to take my advice.

In hindsight, it's not just obvious what you should have done; it's simple. Unfortunately, results are *not* retroactive. If they were, my job would be very easy, and I'd always be right. The average investor sees that they are putting their life savings into an asset allocation (no matter how conservative) and chooses to see it as if they are gambling. I've heard this throughout my entire career. Even clients of ten-plus years who should know better. In many cases, these clients had advisors who were much too aggressive and got hurt because their goals and objectives were not in alignment with their tolerance for risk. So they are always on the defense and afraid, or they choose not to believe the facts.

Opportunity, or the point for maximum potential, is usually where it's the most painful to invest because the markets are down. In contrast, the point of maximum financial risk is when markets are running high (with no pullback for some time), and many investors are not just optimistic but they are euphoric. To be successful, you must think like an investor and not like a speculator or gambler.

During the financial crises of 2007–2008, a client came to my office for a portfolio review and discussion about the market. This gentleman was a physician and quite astute. He was upset that the market went down so much and in such a short time. He was angry I didn't call him to suggest we should go to cash before the markets declined. I was flattered that he thought I was able to predict the future so easily. Truth is, if I was *that* good (and nobody is, regardless of what they tell you), I would just have provided him the winning lottery numbers for the following week. He was adamant that

I should have seen this coming and done something about it. When I asked him if he sold his home in the past few months, he looked puzzled by my comment. I quickly added that I did not sell mine either, and I wouldn't have expected him to. I did ask why nobody told him (or me) that the real estate market was going to go down (-30 to -50 percent) during the crises and suggest he should have sold when it was at a peak (as you can see, I have a way with words). He got even more upset and said his home is not an investment and asked what my point was. I challenged his statement and said, "Your home is very much an investment. In fact, for many, it's then largest investment they have." I added, "You can always rent, but we choose to buy because it adds value to your overall investment portfolio."

My point is that nobody has a crystal ball, and being an investor does not mean you time the financial markets. Yes, you may get it right once in a while, even a broken clock is right twice a day, but that doesn't make you or your advisor a rocket scientist. I have said it many times in this book and will continue to say it, "Investing is a long-term commitment, and although you should hold for long-term periods, you should also tweak and adjust your portfolio along the way to stay on course."

Many believe airplanes fly point-to-point in a straight line. That's not true at all. When there is a crosswind, which there usually is, the pilot will angle the aircraft into the wind to keep the plane moving along the desired path. It's known as crabbing, and like portfolio management, it requires constant adjustments.

Take advantage of downturns to adjust your portfolio and keep it on course. Don't be afraid to buy low and sell high instead of what too many do when they let their emotions get in the way, which is buy high and sell low.

Chapter 21

"Forget the large-cap growth portfolio—that's doing great. I hate the large-cap value portfolio, and we need to put everything into large-cap growth"

One of the most exciting developments to investing was the creation of ETFs (Exchange Traded Funds). For you history buffs, the very first one was created in Canada in 1990, and in the United States, the first ETF was launched in 1993. I've devoted chapter 32 to discuss ETFs in detail.

ETFs allowed an advisor or portfolio manager to have various styles of equities in a single portfolio (that's explained in chapter 33). Since 1989, I've changed my practice to fee-based using independent money managers to handle the investments. I would create the asset allocation and choose the money managers with my client. Managers were chosen not only for their historic performance but for the specific style of stocks and bonds they would manage (growth, value, large cap, mid cap, small cap, etc.). Each money manager would have a separate account and not be comingled with the others. To achieve proper diversity, it wasn't uncommon for a client to have three to five different managers in their overall portfolio. All assets for the client were aggregated, so a client wasn't penalized and charged a higher fee because they had multiple money managers and multiple accounts.

It may seem like a simple concept, and it generally is to an experienced financial advisor, but to many clients, it created their own competition between accounts and dictated which style they liked better at any given time based solely on performance of each manager. It created emotions for the client, and they would inevitably dictate their actions, regardless of how wrong their thinking was.

Correct asset allocation is the use of many styles of management to hedge one another and therefore reduce overall risk. Think sports for a moment. Not every player on a team plays the same position, and each player is not necessarily as good as some of the other players. But together, they create a team, and each person on the team has a specific purpose. What sports and asset allocation have in common is how we may feel about certain players or components of a portfolio at different times. Have you ever watched a batter come up to the plate at a crucial time in the game (maybe bottom of the ninth with two outs and bases loaded) and you hold your breath and hope they don't strike out? It's no different with using various styles of investment management to create a portfolio. While there will always be one or two styles in your portfolio that seem to be underperforming the others, collectively they have their role in the overall portfolio and complete the entire picture.

When you choose various styles, you want their correlation to be low or at least not the same. For definition, *correlation* is "a number between -1 and +1 calculated to represent the dependence of the two variables." Styles generally don't move up or down the same, and some assets like bonds move in the opposite direction to stocks (possibly -0.75 to stocks in general as an example).

From 1998 through March 2000, large-cap growth was leading performance over large-cap value by a huge amount (this was just prior to the tech bubble). Growth outperformed value by better than 2 to 1. On March 10, 2000, the NASDAQ began to spiral downward and proceeded to decline by (-75%) ending March 2003. During that same period, large-cap value was down approximately (-32%). The S&P 500 was down approximately -50 percent.

Prior to March 10, 2000, I cannot tell you how many clients were telling me how much they hated large-cap value—not just dislike, they really despised value at the time—and they wanted to be 100 percent in large-cap growth. It's a good thing I'm pig-headed and wouldn't back down from my convictions. I convinced them to stay diversified, and it saved them much grief (and money). Not every client had the same allocation. For example, if a client had an allocation of 50 percent large-cap growth and 50 percent large-cap value, they would have been down significantly less than if they were invested 100 percent large-cap growth.

When a portfolio declines by (-50%) the reciprocal to get back to even is +100 percent. This may seem like an unattainable amount, but the average historic time it takes to get back to even is only about 4 and a half years. However, when a portfolio goes down -75 percent, the reciprocal to get back to even is +400 percent. I can tell you from experience that is *not* going to happen anytime soon. In chapter 36, we will discuss sequence of returns when taking cash flow for income and the impact it can have on recovery during very volatile times.

Having diversity among various styles provides downside protection. Don't dislike a particular style just because it's out of favor. As mentioned, each style has a part to play in the overall construction of your portfolio.

Chapter 22

"I don't care that the markets are all down this year. I refuse to spend less—this is my lifestyle. You don't understand"

If you choose to read only one chapter from this book, this is it.

During my thirty-five-year career, I've had the misfortune of watching a few clients run out of money not because of poor performance or because I didn't constantly warn them of the inevitable. They ran out of money because they refused to adjust their spending habits and take advice to cut back. I always got the same response: "You don't understand. I need to (fill in the spending need)." Truth is, I do understand. It's all about simple math, and math doesn't lie.

When people retire with a large sum of money—a lump-sum retirement distribution, sale of their home (scaling down), proceeds from an insurance benefit when a spouse dies, sale of a business, etc.—many never plan correctly and spend as if the money will replenish itself automatically. I've seen too many clients spend above their means by buying very expensive cars, taking elaborate vacations excessively, joining a concierge medical practice (where you do not need an appointment and pay a high annual fee for the service), giving their kids and grandchildren excessive amounts of money, etc. only to find out in a few years that they are on the verge of running out of money. Unfortunately, at that point, it's too late to do anything.

Is there a simple way to structure a plan? Of course, there is. That's why this chapter is so very important. Chapter 36 will go into more detail on creating a cash flow statement to help you plan for success and avoid stress in your retirement. So let's get to it.

I'm going to start with the not-so-magic answer and then give you all the supporting data and information so it makes sense to you. To give yourself a 95 percent chance (sorry, but nothing is 100 percent) of *not* running out of money during your lifetime, you need to keep your annual spending to *4 percent of your investable assets* (4 percent is the number used at the time of retirement and based on the assets you have at retirement. Increase the amount annually for inflation using the current years inflation number). I don't want to scare you, but the number is actually slightly less than 4 percent, but it's okay to start with 4 percent. Also, investable assets do *not* include your home (read chapter 29 on reverse mortgages if most of your net worth is tied up in the equity of your home), cars, jewelry, clothing, artwork, and anything else outside of cash and liquid investments.

Let me put this into real numbers so it makes better sense (or depresses you). If your investments are $1,000,000 at the time of your retirement (or the time you choose to stop working), you must limit your spending to 4 percent annually, or $40,000. If inflation is 2.50 percent the following year, you can take $41,000 ($40,000 + 2.50%

= $41,000) and so on. We will go over where to take the income from later in this chapter, so don't get ahead of things. Remember when becoming a millionaire was a dream? Unfortunately, with historic inflation and rising costs of living, a million dollars isn't what it used to be—another reason why investing is so important.

Here's a sad fact: Where taking a 4 percent annual distribution gives you a 95 percent chance of not running out of money, increasing that amount to 5 percent annually gives you an 85 percent chance of running out of money! (This does not include adjusting for inflation each year, which you should.) This is very serious and not to be taken casually.

To be clear, taking a 4 percent distribution annually doesn't mean you will not go into your principal. It means you have a 95 percent chance of not running out of money. The depression generation was fixated on not going into principal (rightfully so), but interest rates were significantly higher prior to 2007 (even though inflation was also much higher). For those of us who are baby boomers or younger, accept the fact that going into your principal will not result in your demise.

You must treat your investments the same way you would run a successful business. When business is good (your portfolio is doing very well), splurge a little (within reason). Take that extra vacation you dreamed about and reward yourself for managing your portfolio well. But when business is down (your portfolio is down and not doing as well), like in a recession, cut back and be frugal.

So now let's discuss the data to prove this and make sense of why you should limit your distribution to 4 percent annually. For the examples I am going to use, I will be very aggressive using a portfolio constructed of 100 percent equities/stocks (worst-case scenario). I am absolutely *not* suggesting this type of aggressive allocation for a retiree, regardless of how aggressive you are as an individual. Your financial advisor will help you determine a proper asset allocation—this is just for example and information purposes.

The historic average time it takes for the S&P 500 to go from a bottom back to its peak is four and a half years (yep, that's all it takes, but most investors get out at the bottom and get back in at the top. See the chart in chapter 1). So let's use a really bad time in modern day, the technology bubble which occurred from March 2000–March 2003. The S&P 500 declined (-46.55%).

What we are going to discuss are two things that will make all the difference in the world:

1. Sequence of returns
2. Sequence of distributions

S&P 500 Annual Returns
(January 1, 2000–December 31, 2006)

YEAR	PERFORMANCE
2000	(-10.14%)
2001	(-13.04%)
2002	(-23.37%)
2003	+26.38%
2004	+8.99%
2005	+3.00%
2006	+13.62%

Sequence of Returns

Sequence of returns is simply annual returns and the sequence (annually) you get them. What's interesting is, if you take any number of years investing and add the performance, the end result always comes out exactly the same, regardless of what order you put the returns in. Let's use the example from the chart above.

If you started investing January 1, 2000, and ended December 31, 2006, your total return was

(-10.14) + (-13.04) + (-23.37) + 26.38 + 8.99 + 3.00 + 13.62 = +5.44%

Now let's mix up the years and see where you end:

8.99 + 13.62 + (-13.04) + 26.38 + (-10.14) + 3.00 + (-23.37) = +5.44%

Do this in any order, and the end number will always be the same. However, start taking money out for distributions, and we embark on a very different journey.

Sequence of Distributions

Sequence of distributions applies to when you start taking money from your portfolio. This is when your portfolio will be greatly impacted by how much you take out and can be the difference between success and running out of money.

Let me give you some basic math to make the point, and then we will go into specifics. If you have one hundred dollars, and it declines by 50 percent, you now have fifty dollars. To get back to one hundred dollars, the reciprocal return you need is 100 percent ($50

+ 100% return = $100). Remember, you didn't take any distributions. For simplicity, let's say you took out twenty-five dollars during the decline. So you started with one hundred dollars and it declined 50 percent, hence the fifty dollars. And then you withdrew another twenty-five dollars, so you have twenty-five dollars left. To get back to one hundred dollars, you must have performance of 400 percent ($25 + 400% = $100)! I am going to be brutally honest—that's not going to happen anytime soon.

Now, let's use real numbers with the same example of the S&P 500 above from January 1, 2000–December 31, 2006:

S&P 500 Annual Returns (January 1, 2000–December 31, 2006) Starting with $100 and Equal Distributions from Starting Amount at 4% Annually (Without Inflation)

YEAR	START VALUE	PERFORMANCE	4% DISTR.	END VALUE
2000	$100	(-10.14%)	$4	$85.86
2001	$85.86	(-13.04%)	$4	$70.66
2002	$70.66	(-23.37%)	$4	$50.15
2003	$50.15	+26.38%	$4	$59.38
2004	$59.38	+8.99%	$4	$60.72
2005	$60.72	+3.00%	$4	$58.54
2006	$58.54	+13.62%	$4	$62.51

I am certain that looking at the chart above, you are probably saying to yourself, "Wait a minute, I'm still down almost 40 percent! This is nuts. I can't even take 4 percent for distributions." Although

I cannot dispute that, I also stopped at December 31, 2006. Even though we had another major decline in 2008, the S&P 500 ended December 31, 2006, (see above chart) at 1,418 and by December 31, 2017, it was at 2,673. That's an additional +88 percent return.

I realize this isn't perfect, as nothing is, but the goal is to make sure you do not run out of money during your lifetime. And this is only taking a 4 percent distribution. Do the math on where you would be if you are taking out 5 percent or 6 percent—scary.

To also want to remind you that a few paragraphs back, I did say (in case you missed it, I will copy and paste it here):

> For the examples I am going to use, I will be very aggressive using a portfolio constructed of 100 percent equities/stocks (worst-case scenario). I am absolutely *not* suggesting this type of aggressive allocation for a retiree, regardless of how aggressive you are as an individual. Your financial advisor will help you determine a proper asset allocation—this is just for example and information purposes.

If the advisor suggests being this aggressive, please go right to chapter 30. Your advisor should recommend a more conservative allocation with a good portion of the allocation in fixed income for stability and safety.

Chapter 23

"I don't want to lose $3,000! I would rather buy a Chanel dress"

This was one of my first experiences with how to define risk with a different paradigm. It was also early in my career with a soon-to-be client who was referred by another good client. This couple would also soon become one of my biggest clients at the time.

I was at their home, and we were discussing asset allocation and goals. The accounts were with a competitor, and they wanted to transfer their assets to me to manage. While discussing the ups and down of the market, the wife confidently stated, "I don't want to lose $3,000! I would rather buy a Chanel dress." Really? Seriously? I didn't know how to respond as I was never posed a statement like that before. Candidly, my initial reaction was that it was a ridiculous request. Markets don't only move in one direction, and they do experience pullbacks. Thinking about the midseven figures they were asking me to manage and the likelihood of losing more than $3,000 on any given down day, how can I possibly accept and agree to a request like this? Anyone who knows me knows that I am never short on words. But this time, I really didn't know what to say or how to answer.

I then realized that her comment had something very similar in common with my wife's thought process on losing money. Don't stop reading yet, because although their thought process was similar, my wife doesn't wear Chanel dresses and, at the time, my bank account wasn't even remotely close to the amount they were giving me to manage. If I go to a casino with friends and lose money, it generally doesn't bother me because I am having fun and being entertained. Don't get me wrong. It's much more fun to come home a winner, and I try not to make a habit out of losing money. I just think of it the same way as going to a show or out for a good dinner. It's all about having fun and being entertained. My wife would understand how I feel, but she won't gamble and doesn't like throwing money away, even for fun. She would rather use the money to buy something for our kids, our home, us, or to go on a vacation. She views gambling as a risk she won't take. Smart woman I married, right?

Everyone has their own definition of risk and how they view it. As an advisor, I have to look into what they are saying and translate it to investing. Keep in mind, investments are intangible, and you can't really touch or feel them. When someone describes their tolerance for risk or pain, it's good to put it in a tangible sense so it's easier to understand.

Since that time, I have used an example of driving out to the Grand Canyon. For some, once they see a sign that says "Grand Canyon—Exit 20 miles ahead," they will start to sweat profusely. For others, they will be exhilarated hanging off the side of the canyon by their fingertips. Who is to say what is the right reaction?

One of the biggest issues with defining risk is taking a level that *you* want, not what other people expect you to take. Risk is purely individual and should coincide with your expectations for returns too. Of course, we all want the highest returns possible. But how much downside are you willing to risk to get there? It should be a healthy balance that you can live with during bad times so you are able to stay with your plan to experience the good times too.

Oh, and this client? I really liked her analogy about comparing buying an expensive dress to risk, and it got me thinking about approaching it with my clients in a different way. Instead of using percent return (up and down), I ask them to define risk in any way that is meaningful to them (tangibly). This client did me a very big favor by showing me a better way to help people understand risk.

Chapter 24

"I know we are only 50 percent in stocks and overall we are doing okay, but I can't stand looking at the market every day. It makes me crazy"

I remember hearing a story about a guy who would come home every night from work and put his hand on his wife's right shoulder. The problem was, she had severe sensitivity in her right shoulder, and every time he did it, she would scream in pain. So my question is, How insensitive (or dumb?) can he be that he keeps touching her right shoulder? (I know it's a made-up story, but if it wasn't, she should try to get him into therapy because there is obviously something wrong.)

So to counter the statement "I know we are only 50 percent in stocks, and overall, we are doing okay, but I can't stand looking at the market every day. It makes me crazy," why do they keep looking at the market as if they are 100 percent invested in stocks? The client also acknowledged they are doing okay, so it's really just how they see the market and what it means to them.

I believe these clients, like many, are viewing the stock market as a mecca for legalized gambling. It's not. Proper investing is no different than owning a business. Think about it, when you buy stocks, you are actually buying shares in existing companies and their existing management teams. These are the same companies you frequent and buy goods from every day. If you order a product from Amazon or buy a computer from Apple, do you think you are actually gambling on your purchase? If the product isn't good or doesn't work, won't they take it back?

Look at the things you buy and where you buy them from. Have you ever wondered if those companies are public and trade on an exchange so you can buy shares? If they are, and most likely they are, are you really gambling? Peter Lynch, one of the world's best and well-known money managers (he managed the Fidelity Magellan fund in their heyday back in the '80s), used to go shopping with his wife and observe what consumers bought. Many of the companies that made those products he bought and included in his mutual fund. Do you think he believed he was gambling by doing so?

Think about this: if you invest just a few hundred dollars or a few hundred thousand dollars and buy a diversified vehicle like a mutual fund or ETF (see chapter 32), you are buying pieces of all the companies held in that mutual fund or ETF. In essence, you may own a small piece of hundreds or thousands of companies. Can you be more entrepreneurial?

Many successful people own their own business. Do you think when they get up in the morning to go to their place of business, they say to themselves, "I hope today I make the right bets on what we will do." They may say, "I hope I make many great decisions today and I make a lot of money," but I would doubt they are looking at their businesses as gambling.

It's all about changing your paradigm. If you think you are gambling and treat it as such, then you probably are. Do you think every time Warren Buffett takes a position in a company, he is thinking about gambling or looking to get out if it goes up slightly? Not at all. Investing is long-term, and long-term is a lot longer than it will take you to finish reading this paragraph.

If you reread the client's comment, they say, "I know we are only 50 percent in stocks…" Throughout this book, a common thread is having an asset allocation you are comfortable with that coincides with your goals, tolerance for risk, and objectives. This is the foundation to build upon so you can get through rough periods in the financial markets. Know what percentage exposure you have to the market before you look at your portfolio after a great day or a bad day. Know that stocks and bonds don't usually move together in the same direction (low correlation), so if your stocks are down, your bonds may be up slightly or flat. If the markets have a really bad day and are down (-2.00%) and you are 50 percent in the market, simple math will tell you that you should be down approximately (-1.00). I say *should* because things aren't always perfect and would work as they should. There are days you may be down worse or up more, but this will give you a good metric to work from. Before you look at your portfolio (it's okay to admit you check your account value online every day), in your mind, come up with where you should be. Unless you are invested 100 percent in stocks, you should be pleasantly surprised that you are not down nearly as much as you think.

Stop being a gambler with your investments, and think like the entrepreneur and investor you really want to be.

Chapter 25

"I know interest rates are at all-time lows. I can't take the volatility of the stock market. I'm putting everything into bond funds"

If interest rates are low (or low by historical standards) and they are poised to rise, going into bond funds would be similar to bungee jumping without having a bungee cord attached to your body. When you finally land, expect lots of pain.

Before we get started, let's discuss what an individual bond is and what a bond fund is.

What Is a Bond?

An individual bond is a fixed income vehicle created by the Government (US Treasuries), a municipality (muni bonds), or corporation (corporate bonds). The easiest way to look at it is to think of a bond as an IOU between the lender and the borrower. When Governments or corporations need to raise money to finance projects or refinance existing debts, bonds are created and issued. The consumer, or borrower, purchases bonds through a securities firm and, in essence, is loaning the lender/issuer money (the bond). In return, the issuer will pay the borrower a set interest rate semiannually (known as the coupon) until the bond matures (maturity or end date), at which time they will give them back the principal (known as par value, or $1,000 per bond). As I will discuss below, bonds trade daily, and their principal values will fluctuate as interest rates change.

What Is a Bond Fund?

A bond fund is a professionally managed pooled investment vehicle made up of individual bonds and other debt instruments. Pooled funds mean it is funded by many investors and sold to investors in shares. Like an individual bond, they are bought and sold through securities firms and generally have daily liquidity (subject to the current price at the time of purchase or sale). If it's a Government bond fund, the fund would invest in Government bonds; if it's a corporate bond fund, it would invest in corporate bonds; and so on. A bond manager, or management team, would manage the fund based upon the written objectives of the fund (in the fund prospectus) and would pay shareholders income monthly. There is no maturity date for a bond mutual fund, and the money manager will make changes on a discretionary basis to the bond holdings as necessary to maintain income and stability where possible.

As I just stated, bond funds (not individual bonds) do not have a maturity. And because there is no maturity, your principal, or amount you invest, is at risk when interest rates fluctuate. Individual bonds also have principal risk prior to maturity, but assuming they do not default, they will mature to par value which is $1,000 per bond. While bonds are typically bought and sold in $5,000 increments, par value for each bond is still $1,000.

Bonds trade daily like stocks, and their principal value will fluctuate as overall interest rates change (not to be confused with the interest rate the bond pays, which is generally fixed and set when the bonds are originally issued). To add a little more confusion, interest rates in general change and move throughout the trading day, just like stocks, and not just when the Government announces an interest rate change. Interest is the cost of borrowing money, and to entice lending, banks will drop their interest rates.

How about a short lesson on interest rates?

The Prime Rate is the rate the nation's top commercial banks charge their best customers. It's also typically uniform from bank to bank. The Federal Funds Rate is the interest rate banks charge one another for overnight loans. The Fed Funds Rate is controlled by the Federal Reserve, and when a rate change is announced, this is what they are referring to. The Federal Reserve will change rates based on impending inflation or recessions. When the Fed feels the economy is getting ahead of itself (too strong), they will raise rates to avoid inflation. Higher interest rates mean higher borrowing costs, so in turn, people will spend less. In contrast, lower rates entice people to borrow more, so consumer spending is increased, which stimulates the economy.

Now back to bonds and bond funds.

Prior to maturity, as interest rates rise, existing bond prices/values fall. When interest rates fall, existing bond prices/values rise. I know this is very confusing. If it makes you feel more human, I also found it very difficult to understand when I studied for my securities licenses, so you are not alone here—I feel your pain.

Let me explain in simple terms why this happens. Let's say you have a bond that has an interest rate of 5 percent, and rates for the same maturity are now at 6 percent. Why should I buy your bond paying 5 percent when I can purchase a new one with the same maturity that's paying 6 percent? The owner of the 5 percent bond (or bond trader for the firm you are buying it from) would adjust the current purchase price lower (maybe $960 or so). Between the interest rate and current purchase price combined, the yield to maturity would come out to the current rate (or 6 percent). Remember, the bonds will still mature to $1,000, so you will get the interest payments semiannually (that's typically how bonds pay interest) until the bond matures and the capital appreciation (the difference of what you paid for the bond and the maturity value of $1,000). Don't worry about having to figure this all out—the market will do it for you.

Just keep in mind that as the bond gets closer to maturity, the principal value will change and adjust daily. If you paid a premium, that premium will dissipate; if you bought it at a discount (a lower current interest rate), the bond value will increase to par. Why would you buy a bond at a premium? Possibly because you want a higher current income (interest rate), so you will forgo some principal (premium paid) to get the added income.

But this chapter is about bond funds (not individual bonds), so let's go back to why bond mutual funds are not a good investment in a rising-rate environment. One thing many investors may argue in defense of bond funds is, "They pay a great interest rate and provide monthly income." That may be true, but be skeptical that it's odd for someone to give away dollar bills for fifty cents without a catch. If the current interest rates are around 4 percent, how can a bond fund be paying 5 percent or 6 percent? Typically, there are only a few reasons:

- The fund may use leverage (typically, this is not the case, but it is a possibility). If this is the situation, the fund takes on significant additional risk as interest rates rise. Ask yourself, Did you buy the fund for income or speculation?
- The fund may be holding lower quality bonds (not investment grade bonds but possibly holding some junk-rated bonds). It's important to note that bond funds typically hold many different bonds from multiple issuers and are generally very diversified. Bond defaults are not very common, so this, too, may not be a major concern. However, in the past, even investment-grade bonds have defaulted; one example is Washington Public Power Supply System (WPPSS), which were AAA rated but failed during the 1980s. Because of the typical diversity within a bond fund, even if a default happens, it shouldn't be catastrophic to the overall fund.
- The fund buys bonds with long maturities. *This is usually the situation* and poses significant risk when rates are low and rising.

The longer the maturity of the bonds held in the fund, the more volatility the fund will experience when interest rates change. To put this perspective, a 1 percent rise in interest rates on a thirty-year bond could result in a principal loss of (-20 to -30 percent). Many long-term bond funds hold bonds with maturities this long, so beware. Because bond funds do not have a maturity, there is no guarantee that your principal value will return either.

I was on vacation in London toward the latter part of the financial crises in 2009 and started a conversation with a gentleman who was on one of the excursions we took. He was on his phone checking on the happenings in the financial markets. He told me that he wasn't worried at all because his portfolio was mostly income producing long-term bonds and preferred stocks and that he was getting a very high yield. To refresh your memory, during the financial crises of 2008–2009, short-term interest rates were almost 0 percent and long-term bonds were only paying a few percent return annually. I couldn't help myself and asked him if he was aware that when rates rise, he can potentially lose 20 percent or more of his principal. He said he wasn't worried, and I wasn't going to push the situation. But if you get an income of 4 percent to 5 percent and lose 20 percent of your principal because of rising rates, doesn't that mean you have a loss of -15 percent? It's simple math, and math doesn't lie.

I remember a prospect in 1987 who had a high-quality Government bond fund. He couldn't understand why he lost so much principal as rates rose. Just because it was a high-quality Government fund doesn't mean it wouldn't be subject to volatility when rates change.

In defense of bond funds, if interest rates are high, bond funds aren't so bad. That's because when rates decline, your principal will actually grow. But there is no maturity, so your income over time will also decline. Personally, I would rather buy individual bonds and know what I'm getting.

So what's the answer? It always comes back to having an allocation between stocks and bonds that is coincidental with your risk tolerance. Just because the stock market is down is not a reason to get out and go to bonds 100 percent. Stocks are the best hedge against inflation, and proper diversification between stocks and bonds is crucial to success. I would also encourage you to always buy high-quality bonds (especially if you are risk adverse) and stay away from bond mutual funds. If an interest rate sounds too good to be true, it usually is, and there's more to it than what's on the surface. Create a plan, and stick to it.

Chapter 26

"I'm not going to invest in a portfolio made up of ETFs—I did that already, and it doesn't work"

Just because you drove a car that had lots of mechanical problems, it doesn't mean all cars are terrible and you should buy a scooter or go-cart instead. There is a tremendous difference between a Ferrari and a Yugo (at the risk of dating myself, the Yugo was a small and quite ugly car that was a huge automotive failure made in Yugoslavia).

ETFs, or Exchange Traded Funds (see chapter 32 for full description), are market indexes that trade like stocks. There are literally thousands available and will mimic the index, or a variation of an index, they are meant to follow. They are generally not managed (passive), although some ETFs are being managed. In my opinion, ETFs are one of the greatest products to come along since mutual funds. Since statistically 75 percent of all portfolio managers do not beat their respective index, why not just buy the index? Also, internal fees on many ETFs are the lowest of any product in the financial industry. A financial advisor can suggest a combination of various ETFs (and other vehicles) to create a diversified portfolio that is suitable to your goals, tolerance for risk, and objectives. Using various styles and classes of indexes offers diversity and is covered in chapter 33 (Modern Portfolio Theory, or MPT).

If you went to one hundred different financial advisors all using ETFs, you will more than likely have one hundred different results (unless a few of those advisors are with the same firm and are using the same firm-designed model). Remember, it's the advisor that is putting your plan together and suggesting the diversity of the investments, and most do not think alike and have their own opinions.

Most great investment vehicles can be bad if you buy them for the wrong reasons or have the wrong expectations. A bad experience shouldn't tarnish your thinking about one or two specific investment vehicles.

During the course of my career, I've had many clients refuse to even discuss certain strategies because of a bad experience they once had. In situations like this, they really miss out on strategies that would really benefit them. There really isn't much more for me to say about this except you should be open-minded and hear and read all you can about something before you make a final decision.

Chapter 27

"I will only do annuities because there is nothing better" or "I will not do annuities because of what I heard"

Annuities are something you either love or hate. Many dislike annuities because many don't fully understand them, and even those that love them don't necessarily understand them fully.

What is an annuity? For this discussion, we will talk about annuities sold by insurance companies or securities firms licensed in insurance. (I do not want to confuse the insurance annuity product with receiving an annuity payment from your company-defined benefit pension plan when you retire. There may be similarities, but I want to keep this simple.) The two basic types of annuities are fixed and variable. Both types generally offer specific guarantees. There are many variations of variable annuities based on what it is invested in, but for simplicity, I will use a choice of mutual funds for the investments.

Much like a qualified retirement plan, such as an IRA, the annuity will grow tax-deferred (until you take funds out). In after-tax accounts (nonretirement accounts), distributions are taxed as income using the earnings first method (LIFO, or "last in, first out"). Years ago (unfortunately, it's no longer done this way), the taxation method for distributions was calculated as principal first, so there was no tax until all principal was distributed first (FIFO, or "first in, first out"). There are no capital gains in an annuity, so all distributions are taxed at your income tax rate.

In essence, buying an annuity is similar to having another retirement plan because of the tax-deferred treatment. But like a retirement plan, any taxable distributions made prior to the owner turning fifty-nine and a half years old will also result in an additional 10 percent tax penalty. When you add this 10 percent penalty to the Federal and State income tax that will be due, taking distributions prior to fifty-nine and a half can result in a large tax bill. That's one reason not to purchase an annuity in a personal, after-tax account prior to being close to age fifty-nine and a half—or if you absolutely know you will not touch those funds until you are older than fifty-nine and a half. It's also always a good idea to seek tax advice from a tax professional first.

The biggest benefit I see in an annuity is the guarantee of principal. Let's say you have $200,000 in your investments, and you split the money by putting $100,000 in an S&P 500 Index, and the other $100,000 in a variable annuity. Right after doing this, the S&P 500 declines significantly, and each investment is now worth $50,000 each ($100,000 total). Unfortunate for you, the stress physically kills you. Where the S&P 500 index is now only worth $50,000, upon your death the annuity will be restored to a minimum of what you put in, or $100,000 (minus anything you may have taken out; for this example, we will assume nothing was taken out). Sorry, but this benefit goes to your beneficiary, and you won't live to see it. Yes, you must die for this guarantee to go into effect. Some annuities also offer step-up guarantees based on annual performance, and it is important to look in to that too prior to purchase.

Many advisors may recommend buying an annuity in your IRA or retirement plan. You may be thinking, *Why would I put a tax-deferred vehicle (annuity) in another tax-deferred vehicle (IRA)? Where is the benefit?* The only benefit of buying an annuity in your IRA is the death benefit as I described in the paragraph above. For me, that's the only reason to buy an annuity in a retirement plan. If not for the death benefit, why would I pay the extra fees? (Don't worry, we will discuss fees in detail a little further down in this chapter.)

Buying an annuity does *not* mean you are or you have to annuitize it. In fact, in most cases, that is something you do not want to do. What does annuitizing mean anyway? Annuitization is the process of converting an annuity into periodic income payments that are guaranteed for the annuitant's life or the annuitant's life with a guaranteed specified period of time. An example with a guaranteed specified period of time is this: the annuity will pay a specific amount of income for the life of the annuitant with a period certain of ten years (it can also be five years or twenty years, depending on what the insurance company offers). That means if the annuitant dies within that ten-year period, it will continue to pay the annuitant's beneficiary the same income for the remainder of that ten-year period. If the annuitant lives beyond the ten years, it will continue to pay the set amount of income until the annuitant dies, regardless of age.

Once you annuitize, you give up ownership of the principal in place of guaranteed periodic payments, as described above. You heard that correct, and this is why I do not like annuitization. However, a key benefit if you choose to annuitize is, you cannot outlive an annuity. So if your family history shows everyone living to 150 years, maybe annuitizing isn't a bad choice? Also, if you are not worried about keeping your principal or do not have any beneficiaries, then annuitization may be a worthwhile choice to consider.

If you choose *not* to annuitize, the owner has the ability to take distributions, even before the penalty period is over. Many annuity distribution allowances are different, so verify with the specific annuity you are thinking about purchasing prior to purchase for the allowable amount. When you take distributions—whether monthly, quarterly, annually, or one-time periodically—that is not annuitizing; it's just a distribution. If you elect to annuitize, generally you will be offered a higher than normal distribution (income) rate because, as I stated above, once you annuitize, you give up the rights to the principal.

So what is a fixed annuity, and how does it differ from a variable annuity? A fixed annuity is very simple because it offers a fixed rate of return that is locked in for the duration of the annuity contract. It's much like a CD, but an annuity grows tax-deferred where the CD is taxable as interest is paid. When the fixed-rate guarantee ends, you can do what is called a 1035 tax-free exchange into another annuity. However, the penalty period for early termination will start again, so just be aware.

A variable annuity is an annuity that is invested in various investments, like mutual funds. (There are many varieties of variable annuities, such as index annuities and others, but for this example, I will use mutual funds for the investments.) The results/performance of this type of annuity will be based on the performance of the investment choices held. Typically, there are many investment choices to choose from, including predetermined asset allocation funds, to make it easier for the investor to match their tolerance for risk. You can also switch between the funds offered without additional fees or penalties. As your goals, objectives, and tolerance for risk change, you are not locked into your original choices and can make the necessary adjustments. You also can take distributions monthly, quarterly, semiannually, annually, or as needed penalty-free up to the allowable annual amount stated in the contract. A variable annuity will offer the potential for higher growth, but based on the underlying investments, you will also be taking more risk. Because variable annuities offer investments instead of having a fixed rate of return, they also come with much higher fees.

Fees are generally very high in variable annuities because of the underlying investments that are responsible for the potential for higher returns. Other fees such as insurance costs, mutual fund management fees, administrative costs, etc. contribute to the high annual costs that will reduce your net performance results. You also pay insurance costs to add the guarantees. Remember, the name insured *(the annuitant)* must die for that guarantee to happen.

Based on the class of annuity you buy, you can have a high upfront charge (maybe as high as 8 percent or more), or instead of an upfront fee, you'll have a back-end penalty if you close it out during the first seven-plus years. Every annuity fee structure is different, so be sure to fully understand this prior to any purchase.

There is quite a bit more to understanding annuities, but rather than overwhelm you, I chose to just provide the key, important facts.

Annuities very much have their place in investing and portfolio construction. They just aren't for everyone. When using an advisor, keep an open mind. Like any investment strategy, if they suggest annuities, ask why is it being recommended and how will it benefit you. Don't just say no because of what you heard or what your immediate impression is. Look deeper before concluding. I would say that for any recommended investment strategy.

Chapter 28

"I just received a notice for a Class Action Lawsuit. Am I being sued?"

No, you are not being sued, so no worries.

A Class Action (for securities) is a lawsuit brought about by a group of investors who bought or sold a company's securities during a specific period of time and suffered losses as a result of violations of the securities laws. In more simple terms, it allows you as an investor to participate in a group lawsuit against a public company (a company that trades on a Securities Exchange), and you may be entitled to share in the settlement (if it's settled, but not all are).

You do not need to be the person who originated the lawsuit. The law firm(s) handling the class action will notify all investors that held the security and provide forms that will need to be competed to participate. Keep in mind that it's not mandatory that you participate. If you choose not to participate, you will also not share in any settlement (after legal fees and other expenses).

Typically, you will have to provide the dates you purchased and sold the specific securities along with the number of shares you held.

You may even have to provide statements or confirmations as proof. This is all outlined on the form sent to you.

Many securities firms will *not allow* their financial advisers to complete these forms on behalf of their clients, so you will likely have to do it yourself if you choose to participate. Over the past few years, some brokerage firms created a process you can sign up for that will automatically include you in any class action suits, and you will not have to do anything. If available, this is definitely something you should take advantage of. You may want to inquire with your adviser to see if their firm participates in such a service.

Keep in mind that settlements can sometimes take years before any payments are actually made. The amount you *may* receive will depend on the amount of shares you held (total investment) and the amount of any loss (or gain) you may have had. You may also not be entitled to get anything.

Remember, it is a shared settlement among all the participants, and the lawyers handling the class action tend to do quite well (for doing all the work), so I wouldn't suggest buying that ski condo you've had your eye on just yet.

Chapter 29

"I would never do a reverse mortgage. I don't want to give up ownership in my home"

So many people, including many financial professionals, have misconceptions about reverse mortgages. I must admit, so did I until I had to get certified to do one for my mom after my dad passed away in 2006.

Taking a reverse mortgage does *not* mean you give up ownership or annuitize your home in any way. In fact, it's a nonrecourse loan. By definition, that means it is a secured loan that is secured by a pledge of collateral (your home in this case), but for which the borrower is not personally liable. In simple terms, that means you are using your home as collateral for the loan. If upon the borrower's death, you owe more than the amount of the outstanding loan, the home will go into foreclosure and the estate owes nothing.

There are some rules that must be adhered to in order to apply for a reverse mortgage. The owner or owners must be at least sixty-two years of age, and the home that you are taking the reverse mortgage on must also be the primary residence of the owners. That means they must live there full-time. If one spouse passes away and the surviving spouse goes into an assisted living facility (or if this happens to both spouses), payments cease and the home must be sold and/or the amount owed on the reverse mortgage must be paid off. The home doesn't have to be sold; the beneficiaries have the right to retain ownership but must pay off the reverse mortgage loan. As I stated in the previous paragraph, if the home is valued less than what is owed on the mortgage, the lender takes over and the owner or beneficiaries owe nothing.

All reverse mortgages are backed by the United States Government, and as part of the application process, the owners must also attend a session to council them on all the intricacies of this type of mortgage. It is especially important to fully understand what negative amortization means and the impact it can have. I would advise that another family member attend the session to act as an additional set of eyes and ears so there are no surprises to the beneficiaries of the estate (and subsequently, this home) down the road.

As mentioned, the owners must be at least sixty-two years of age; but the older you are when you apply, the more income you will receive. In other words, you shouldn't do a reverse mortgage at sixty-two years of age unless you do not have enough in savings and investments to sustain your lifestyle. Wait as long as you can because your monthly payments will be more every year you age if you wait, because your life expectancy decreases every year (they use a generous figure for assumed age of death, typically greater than one hundred years old).

Your payments or income from the reverse mortgage are considered a return of your principal (equity) in the home, so there are no taxes due from these payments. You really aren't borrowing money, but instead, you are getting access to your own money (equity in the home) in the form of a monthly payment. The lender is charging you interest on the funds they are giving you to tap into that equity without you having to sell the home. That's how the lender is making money. Unlike a typical first or second mortgage, where you pay the lender every month a combination of interest and principal to repay the loan, the lender pays you each month and charges you interest (interest accrues and compounds) until the loan is paid off (when the owner doesn't live there anymore, dies, or sells the home).

The interest rate charged is generally much higher than a conventional mortgage, and the biggest downside to this type of loan is that it works on negative amortization. That means the interest accrues monthly along with principal payments you are receiving, and you will pay interest on the interest that is accruing on top of the principal. So the outstanding debt on the loan will increase every month. Remember, you are not paying the bank—they are paying you.

There are two ways to do a reverse mortgage to take the principal out of your home: a lump sum or in monthly payments. Personally, I don't think lump-sum payments should be allowed, and I always suggested clients not receive a payment this way. Why? Two reasons. First, taking a lump sum will have a severe negative impact on negative amortization and interest compounding. This is because you are then paying interest on the lump sum or higher balance. Second, typically when the recipient gets a large sum of money, it tends to get spent quickly, and family members suddenly come out of the woodwork asking for financial help for one thing or another. Once the money you receive is gone, that's it. There is no more. You also no longer have any equity in the home. However, you can still live there, but you must continue to pay the insurance, taxes, upkeep, etc. because you still own the home until both mortgagees die or the home is sold. You never give up ownership. Getting paid a monthly amount allows you to "pensionize" your home and receive payments to aid in financing your lifestyle.

Here is the process (it may vary slightly depending on the lending institution):

1. The owners apply for a reverse mortgage (they must be at least sixty-two years old)

2. After completing all necessary documents, the owners attend a counseling session that will be arranged by the lender

3. An appraisal is done on the home, and a monthly payment will be determined by the lender based on the appraisal and life expectancy of the owners

4. Once accepted and completed, the lender will pay off any existing mortgages on the home, which will add to the amount owed along with all closing costs

5. You will receive a monthly check for the lives of the owners*
   a) * If the owners can no longer live there (they go into assisted living or similar and/or die), payments cease and the mortgage must be paid back or the home sold to satisfy the loan due.
      i. Interest will continue to accrue until the home is sold and the loan is paid in full. If the home is valued less than the loan, it will be offered to the beneficiaries, and if they do not want it, it will go into foreclosure.

1. There is no recourse to the owners or estate if the home goes into foreclosure, and the lender will not seek any additional payments from them.

Allow me to use my mom's situation as a real example (with actual numbers).

My dad died in 2006, and by early 2007, my mom needed additional funds to support her lifestyle. She applied and was accepted for a reverse mortgage. This was just prior to the financial crises in 2008, and her home appraised at the height of the market for $235,000 (she lived in a retirement community, and her apartment was completely remodeled and updated). She also owed approximately $70,000 on an existing mortgage. As I mentioned, closing costs are very high in comparison to a conventional loan and were approximately $10,000. She received monthly checks from the reverse mortgage for $550 and would continue to receive the checks regardless of how long she lived, so long as she continued to live there or passed away. You cannot outlive a reverse mortgage; payments are guaranteed by the United States Government until the owner dies or can no longer live there (i.e., assisted living or similar).

When my mom passed away in 2010, it was at the height of the financial crises, and the resale value of her apartment dropped significantly to approximately $75,000. However, because of the monthly payments she received over the years, having to pay off her prior existing conventional mortgage when she did the reverse mortgage, closing costs, and negative amortization, she owed $115,000! As the executor to her estate, I signed all the rights to the lender, and the home went into foreclosure. Her beneficiaries had the right to purchase the home from the lender, but because of the low value of her apartment and the high amount owed on the loan, everyone passed. There was no additional money owed by our family (it's a nonrecourse loan), and we walked away and let it go into foreclosure.

What's interesting to note is that, while my mom was alive, she lived in the home and continued to do everything an owner does—pay taxes, insurance, maintenance, upkeep, etc. That's because she continued to own the home. She also maintained her independence as a homeowner and her quality of life.

If the financial crises of 2008 did not occur and upon her death the home appreciated slightly each year (just keeping pace with inflation), there would have been quite a bit of equity in the home. Remember, the home was appraised for $235,000, and upon her death, the balance owed on the mortgage was $115,000. Had there been no financial crises and the home sold after her death for $235,000, the beneficiaries would have gotten approximately $120,000 (less real estate broker fees and closing costs on the sale). Had she not done the reverse mortgage during her last few years, she would not have been able to maintain her lifestyle, and after her death, the home would still have been valued at $75,000 and the original mortgage debt would have grown to about the same amount (-$75,000) and the beneficiaries would have gotten nothing anyway.

She also didn't just get $550 in monthly income. Because the existing mortgage was rolled into the reverse mortgage, she also saved that mortgage payment (which was approximately $500 a month). In essence, she was saving $1,050 a month not paying the $500 monthly mortgage payment and getting an income of $550 a month.

Many retirees have little to no money in the bank or in investments but own their homes without any debt. In many cases, it's their single largest asset. A reverse mortgage gives them the opportunity to use the equity in their home for additional income (as I suggested, take payments monthly, not in a lump sum). And contrary to what many believe, they *do not* give up their ownership in the home.

Chapter 30

"I'm moving my account (to a competitor) because they can do better"

Sadly, sometimes this is the best solution. Sometimes it's not.

I'm not going to defend anyone or try to sway your thinking, but I will try to possibly have you see it in a different way, because many times, this is an emotional decision.

Are you thinking about a change because of your performance? In many cases, this is the situation. If it's one bad year, is that really fair to the adviser? Maybe it was the result of geopolitical issues, and the advisor just took a more conservative posture. What was their explanation?

Did a friend get under your skin constantly bragging about how amazing her advisor is? Did they tell you their advisor *never* lost money, regardless of how bad the markets were? I heard that quite a few times on the golf course just prior to the financial crises of 2008, and the advisor turned out to be Bernie Madoff. They generally don't give a person 150 years in prison so he can teach the other inmates how to invest properly.

If you think your fees are too high, don't necessarily go by what others pay, because they may not be getting the same level of service you get or the attention to your needs. Even if the fees you pay are higher, how much experience does your advisor have? If you needed an open-heart surgery, are you going to search out the doctor who charges the least, or are you going to look for a doctor with the most experience? How much do you pay your CPA, and how much experience does she have? What amazes me about fees is, some clients will nickel and dime their financial advisor, even though their advisor has made them a lot of money, yet the same clients will go to a restaurant, get abused by the waiter or waitress, eat lousy food, and still leave a 20 percent tip. Seriously? Fees are extremely important in the absence of value. Think about that for a moment.

A relationship should be based on trust. If your life savings was fully invested with an advisor and you got stranded on an island for five years, would you worry that your advisor would do something rogue or unethical that could hurt you? If the answer is yes, then you should absolutely seek another advisor, regardless of how good your performance has been. Trust is everything.

If you decide to go to a new advisor, just expect that the new advisor will suggest that you make changes. Everyone has a different philosophy, and the change could result in large capital gains taxes. If you are not looking for changes, why are you making the change?

Do your homework before you decide and ask yourself, Why do I want to make this change? In many cases, you'll find that you were upset about one or two things in particular, and it may be simple to correct. Isn't it best to have a conversation with your current advisor and be open and honest before you do anything? If the two of you have a good relationship, I think you owe it to yourself and to the advisor. After that conversation, I think the answer will be obvious.

Chapter 31

Identity Theft

Although this was not an actual question from a client, it is a topic I've discussed many times over the years. Identity theft is something most think will never happen to them, even though statistics tell a different story. There are some things you just cannot prevent, but if you prepare properly and take necessary precautions, you can avoid a potential catastrophe. I, too, never thought identity theft would happen to a member of my family, but as John Lennon wrote in a song to his son Sean ("Beautiful Boy") just months before he was senselessly murdered, "Life is what happens to you while you're busy making other plans." I will share my story in detail later in this chapter.

Aside from the typical identity theft we all know of, where someone steals your credit card information through scanners and skimmers or obtaining your Social Security number in various ways, there are other methods as well. Some of these are the following (I will discuss each in detail):

- Phishing
- Smishing

- Vishing
- Pharming
- Kvetching

Phishing

Phishing is done though emails and is disguised as an actual email (a cloned email) from what looks like a real email address or website. The phisher uses real logos and other marks to make it appear legitimate. The phisher attempts to trick the recipient by responding and revealing confidential identifying information (Social Security number, account numbers, usernames, passwords, or other) and then intercepts the response or will ask the recipient log into what looks like a legitimate website but is actually a hyperlink to the phisher's website instead. It is deceptive social engineering. Where it is very difficult to tell a phishing scam, sometimes there are word misspellings or other grammatical errors. If you are not 100 percent sure it's real, do not respond or call the phone numbers listed in the email, as they can be fake as well.

Here's a true story:

Just days after speaking to a client, I received an email request from the client to provide account balances. The email was the client's actual email. They weren't asking for account numbers or anything confidential—just balances. It seemed like a simple request, and because they were not requesting anything confidential like account numbers, it didn't seem like a big deal either. I gathered all the information and typed it all out. Just before I hit Send, something stood out: the client addressed me as Bradley, not Brad. Nobody calls or called me Bradley except my mother, and that was only when she was mad at me about something. So just before I sent it to the client, I decided to call them to verify if they made the request. They were not the one who made the request, and it was a phish! The fix was simple too. I suggested they change their password for their email account and all other accounts for safety. Even though the phisher wasn't asking for confidential information, it could have been the beginning of the scam, and I caught it!

Here's another true story:

A client received an email from my company (his brokerage firm) requesting he follow the attached link to log on and change his expired password. He told me everything in the email looked legitimate (logos, address, phone, etc.) but didn't call me to verify it. Once he clicked the link, he realized he shouldn't have done so and called me. The criminals had access to his accounts and proceeded to move money out of his accounts to their offshore accounts. My company made him whole, and there was no loss for the client. But we had to freeze his accounts, reopen all new accounts and change everything. It took months to complete. By the way, this client is a very successful businessman and holds a Master's Degree. Criminals never discriminate.

Smishing

Smishing is the act of trying to acquire information through cellphone texting methods. The text typically includes a link to click on to verify something. The link allows the criminal access to your cellphone and its contents. The result can be just as catastrophic as a phishing email. Unless you initiated a request, do not respond.

Vishing

Vishing is a scam using the telephone to gain private information. A typical situation is the caller telling you that you have a known virus on your computer and that they can help fix the problem.

Here's a true story:

One of my clients received a call from a "computer company" stating that a known virus was detected on the computer and that it could severely affect the recipient's computer. By giving the caller access to their computer, they could fix the problem easily. I know as you read this, you are doubting someone could be so foolish to allow a stranger who calls access to their computer, but this client was going through some very stressful personal times and was vulnerable. It took months to get the situation resolved and rectified.

Here's another true story:

An elderly person I know received a phone call from someone pretending to be their grandson. When the "grandson" started the call by saying, "Hi, Grandma," the grandmother replied with her grandson's name. Now that the scammer knew the grandson's name, he was able to use it to his advantage during the call. The scammer stated he was in Europe and had a car accident but was okay. He said he needed to pay for the repairs on the rental car right away and if they could wire the money immediately. He added that the person in the repair shop will provide the wire instructions and that they need to go to a Western Union right away to send the funds, or they will not let him leave the repair shop. The scammer begged them not to tell his parents because they would be very upset. The scammer knew they would do what he asked. (Remember, they are elderly, and the call upset them greatly, so they weren't in the mindset to challenge who it really was on the phone.) They were so upset by the call they never thought to call him back on his cellphone, and they just wanted to help him quickly. He knew they wouldn't betray his confidence and call his parents either, so the scam would proceed.

Pharming

Pharming is a cyber attack that redirects a website's traffic to another site. It typically targets a home computer that is unprotected and vulnerable. It can also attack a domain name. If a domain is hijacked, anyone logging in to that website will be directed to the fraudster's fake website.

Kvetching

While *kvetching* isn't really a term used to describe identity theft—it's actually a Yiddish term meaning "to complain or constant complaining"—believe me, if you become a victim of identity theft, you will be doing a lot of kvetching.

Identity theft protection services can help offer additional peace of mind. I am not here to promote one service or another and prefer to remain neutral. There are many good and reliable services available to use. A service will typically notify you immediately through text, email, and a phone call to alert you that someone is attempting to open an account with your information. For the application to complete, you must verify that you initiated the request for credit or/and tell them it's not you, and they will block the application. Choose a service that is aligned with your needs.

Yes, it's another form of insurance that will cost you every year. But like term life insurance or auto insurance, you hope you never need it or get an alert. Do you really want to have an auto accident to get back the money you paid for auto insurance? Do you really want to die before the year ends so your term life insurance pays? That's basically what must happen for you to get paid back. While there is no cash value accumulating for any of these types of policies, what you are buying is peace of mind, and it's a small price to pay.

Another thing you can do, and it costs nothing, is to freeze your credit with the three major credit bureaus. They are Equifax, Experian, and TransUnion. If the credit application cannot access your credit report, chances are, credit will not be granted until the credit is unfrozen and the report can be accessed. While this may not be 100 percent failsafe, coupling freezing your credit with using an identity theft protection service can greatly help prevent identity theft. Just keep in mind that when *you* apply for credit, you must first unfreeze it with the three agencies.

As I mentioned in the first paragraph of this chapter, I want to share what happened to my wife and her/our experience with identity theft. Like most, we never thought it would happen to us. But it did, and I'm very happy that I practice what I preach and had an identity theft protection service.

Someone tried to open a credit card using my wife's Social Security number. From the protection service we have, she received a call, text, and email asking if it was initiated by her. She responded no to the text and immediately received a phone call from the service. They conferenced her in with the credit card company to halt the process of allowing the card to go through. Simple enough, or so we thought.

Weeks later, we received a letter from the Department of Motor Vehicles fraud area because someone requested a duplicate driver's license for my wife. While keeping our actual address on the license, they requested it be mailed elsewhere (an actual home address). You would think the motor vehicle department would immediately notice that doesn't seem correct and not mail it, but guess again. They mailed it to the requested address (I wish I was making this up). We filed a police report to find out that women in their mid- to late fifties were being targeted in our area and all the requests for duplicate driver's licenses were being sent to the same mailing address. You would think the fraud came from the same place, and if it's all going to the same mailing address, an arrest would be made. Think again. Nothing is that simple. The local police said they do not have jurisdiction at the other location and we would have to go to that police department and file a complaint. You really don't have to wonder too hard why identity theft keeps happening!

So what did we do? Exactly what I suggested above. We also added one extra layer of protection. Out of fear that the fraudster would also try to file a fictitious tax return using my wife's Social Security number, we went to the IRS.org and requested that every year, she obtain a security PIN to submit her tax return. I did that for myself as well. That, too, is a free service.

When I decided to add this chapter on identity theft to my book, it was a few months after I completed the initial writing. I realized that risk management (what all forms of insurance is technically called) should include identity theft protection because it's so important. So I started gathering my thoughts and wrote them down as they came to me.

In less than two days of scribbling various notes for this chapter before I actually began writing, I received a frantic call from one of my kids stating that he got an alert on his cellphone that someone tried to open a new credit card with his Social Security number. Yes, my kids are just like me and also use an identity theft protection service. The thief wasn't able to open the card because the service shut down the application immediately. My son then proceeded to freeze his credit with all three of the major agencies I discussed above for his wife and himself.

Identity theft is very real and needs to be taken seriously. It *can* happen to you!

Section 3

The Mystery Solved
for Analysis and
Investing: Just the
Facts

In the next six chapters of this book, I will discuss many of the topics I learned when studying for my CIMA® (Certified Investment Management Analyst®) designation at the Wharton Business School for Executive Education administered through the Investment Management Consultant's Association® (IMCA®), now known as the Investments & Wealth Institute®.

Rather than trying to impress you with verbiage and excruciatingly painful theories and equations, I will cover the topics using very simple and easy-to-understand logic. Understanding these principals and concepts will not take the place of using a financial advisor. It will allow you to work closer with the advisor because of the knowledge and understanding you will gain.

Chapter 32

Simple Three-Step Formula for Success

Let's keep this very simple. There are only three main ingredients for success when investing:

- **Quality**
  - ○ Don't look for shortcuts by buying things of very high risk because you think you can make a huge return in a short period. If something sounds too good to be true, it usually is. If you want to sleep at night, always buy quality.

- **Diversification**
  - ○ Throughout section 2 of this book, I discussed diversification. It's the cornerstone to investing successfully. Modern Portfolio Theory (MPT) is the framework on which to build your portfolio. Introduced in 1952 by Harry Markowitz, he was awarded a Nobel

Prize in Economics for his work. In chapter 33, I discussed Modern Portfolio Theory in detail.

- **Time**
  - This is where too many fail. Time means long-term. And long-term means longer than it takes to write your name. A market cycle used to be considered four to six years. Today, I would consider it to be closer to ten years. However, investing should be a lifelong endeavor. Your goals and tolerance for risk may change, as will your asset allocation, but the concept of investing should be forever.

Expectations

Having reasonable and realistic expectations are key for success. If you think your physical endurance at age eighty is the same as when you were twenty, you are setting yourself up for failure. I'm not saying to stop exercising at eighty. Look at fitness and nutrition expert Jack LaLanne, who was almost ninety-seven years old when he passed away. Sometimes referred to as the godfather of fitness, he always talked about setting reasonable expectations for your fitness routine. Investing is no different. Sometimes, during market pullbacks, even the pain may feel similar as working out. No pain, no gain.

Before you start investing, set up proper expectations based upon the level of risk you are willing to take. That means, downside expectations as well as upside expectations so you can stay with it even during adverse times. Do research and have an in-depth conversation with your financial advisor to establish realistic and reasonable goals and expectations. Set yourself up to win.

Historical Returns

Until March 10, 2000, when the dot-com bubble began its downward spiral and the S&P 500 fell almost (-50%) and the NASDAQ fell considerably more, the historical returns of the markets were 10 percent annually geometric (compounding return) and 12 percent annually arithmetic (simple interest return). Since that time, as of this writing in 2019, the average return of the S&P 500 for the last twenty-five years is around +5 percent annually. Numbers and statistics are rewritten every day, so knowing your numbers will help you when creating proper expectations. See chapter 11 for a full description of historical returns.

What Is Real Rate of Return?

A real rate of return is *not* just how much you make after fees. Some would call that a net, return and stop there. That's only partially true. Getting a satisfactory return on your investments is also about keeping pace with inflation. A *real* return is the bottom-line return *after* all fees, taxes, and inflation. You may have heard the expression, "You would have been better off just keeping your money under your mattress so you wouldn't lose anything." During really bad times in the markets, that's a difficult statement to argue with. However, most things in life aren't retroactive, so having last week's lottery numbers for this week's drawing doesn't really do you much good. If you put a dollar under your mattress for a few years, you may still have a dollar when you retrieve it, but it won't buy you as much as it did when you first put it under your mattress, because the cost of living (inflation) rises every year, and so does prices for goods and services.

The 1980s and the Introduction of No-Load Mutual Funds

The creation of the modern mutual fund dates back to 1924 and was opened to investors in 1928 by a company known today as MFS Investment Management. State Street Investors was the custodian for the fund and later branched out and created their own mutual funds.

During the 1970s no-load funds were created, but they really gained in popularity during the 1980s bull market. During the decade of the eighties, the average return for the S&P 500 was approximately +18 percent annually, yet a large number of no-load investors lost money. (Some would guess that more than 80 percent of no-load investors lost money, but I cannot verify that number, so to be fair, I won't attest to it.) With outstanding average annual returns like this, how could anyone lose money? Simple. There was no cost to get in and out, so emotions took over and caused harm to investors' performance and results (see the emotions chart in section 1). Market timing doesn't work. One of the greatest money managers of all time, Peter Lynch, stated that in his book *One Up on Wall Street*. I fully agree.

Why Many Investors Lose Money?

Just read the two paragraphs above, or pick any chapter through-out sections 1 and 2. It all comes down to emotions and bad decisions. There is a reason why *Behavioral Finance* was awarded multiple Nobel Prizes in Economics.

Behavioral Finance

I'm going to restate what I wrote in section 1, which is also worth rereading:

They say the definition of stupidity is "doing the same wrong things over and over but looking for a different outcome each time." When it comes to investing your hard-earned money, it sounds easy on paper to do the right thing, but in reality, we act on our emotions and typically make the wrong decisions.

Too many people treat investing like gambling, which is a major mistake. It's not gambling! Be an investor and think long-term. Buy quality, have good diversification, and invest for many years, not just a few hours or days.

What Is Long-Term Investing?

Yes, I know it was section 1, but it's that important and worth repeating. As I mentioned above, a market cycle used to be considered four to six years. Today, I would consider it to be closer to ten years. However, investing should be a lifelong endeavor. Your goals and tolerance for risk may change, as will your asset allocation, but the concept of investing should be forever.

Choosing the Proper Level of Risk in the Beginning

Throughout this book, I talked about risk and the importance of taking a level of risk you are comfortable with. This is not an area to rush just so you can get invested quick. Can you imagine a builder constructing a skyscraper and not spending the time to put in a proper foundation? This is an opportunity to work with your financial advisor to define what risk means to you. Don't worry what others think and how they define risk. It's personal and should only be about you. After all, it's your money. Ask yourself, If the market declined by (-50%) as it did during the technology bubble of 2000–2002 and financial crises of 2008, how much downside could I emotionally tolerate before I can't take it any longer and have to get out? Be honest with yourself. If your expectations are to achieve an annual return of +8 percent but you don't want to lose anything during pullbacks, it's not going to happen. You'll have to wait 150 years until Bernie Madoff gets out of jail—and do you really want someone like that managing your life savings? You can always adjust your risk profile, but be realistic. For a pilot, a bad approach usually means a bad landing. That's not the risk you want to take. Define your own risk tolerance and be realistic. Getting through the bad times will allow you to stay for the good ones.

The Dow and the S&P 500 (How Diversified Are They?)

The Dow Jones Industrial Average (Dow) is made up of thirty stocks. The S&P 500 is comprised of five hundred. But how diversified are they really? For the S&P 500, about twelve stocks make up 85 percent of the performance. That may sound hard to believe, but it's because most indexes (and the S&P 500 is one of them) is cap weighted. What does that mean? Funny you should ask. What a perfect segue for the next topic.

What Is Cap Weighting?

Cap weighting, or capitalized weighting, is the weight of each security in an index based upon the total dollar holding of that security on any given day (that's stocks total market value). As a stock's price changes daily, it's weighting in that index changes accordingly. For example, if stock A is being bought by many investors and stock B is being sold by many investors, then stock A will have a higher cap weighting in the index and stock B will have a lesser weighting.

When you look at daily gainers and losers in the market, especially stocks with large percentage moves +/-, this becomes more obvious.

It's important to know that sometimes, the diversity you thought you were getting isn't quite what you thought because of their weightings to the overall index. Most indexes also rebalance periodically (each index is different) to bring things back into alignment.

This is one reason to buy multiple indexes with various styles in your portfolio (see chapter 33 on Modern Portfolio Theory) so you have proper diversification throughout your portfolio.

Chapter 33

What Are ETFs
(Exchange Traded Funds)?

Simply stated, ETFs are index-based mutual funds that trade like stocks on major exchanges. While some ETFs are actively managed and have similar characteristics to mutual funds, the majority of ETFs are passive (nonmanaged).

ETFs have the advantages of index mutual funds but actively trade the same as individual stocks. When buying or selling mutual funds, orders are taken throughout the day, but execution for buys and sells happen after the markets close, regardless of what time the order is placed during the day. ETFs are executed when the order is placed. Pricing is up to the minute and not delayed.

ETFs tend to have very low internal fees and are very cost effective. They will track their respective index closely, offer good diversification, and have strong potential for tax efficiency as well.

Equity ETFs

There are a vast amount of equity ETFs available to choose from. Where many will mimic and track a specific index or sector, some are actively managed, just like their mutual fund cousins. Statistically, many actively managed funds don't even beat their own benchmark, so why not just buy the ETF index that mimics the benchmark. Actively managed mutual funds also tend to have high internal fees.

Because ETFs can be purchased for as little as a single share, it's easy to create a very diversified portfolio inexpensively (Modern Portfolio Theory, see chapter 33). Instead of buying shares of individual companies, buy an ETF index (or sector ETF) that those companies are in and get more diversity (which translates to "safety"). For example, instead of buying shares of Apple, Amazon, Google, and Cisco, why not buy a technology sector ETF that holds all those stocks plus many more companies that are similar and have more diversity?

To see the individual holdings of any ETF, go to the website of the ETF creator (iShares, SPDR, Vanguard, etc.), and you can view all the individual securities within the ETF as well as the weighting for each holding.

Bond (Fixed Income) ETFs

Like equity ETFs, there are a myriad of fixed income ETFs available with varying fixed income characteristics such as bond quality, type of fixed income (corporate, Government, hybrid, or other), and maturity. Unless specified, fixed income ETFs are not derivatives, and the holdings within the ETF are exactly as stated (i.e., a one- to three-year US Treasury ETF will only hold US Treasuries with maturities of one, two, and three years). As each Treasury holding in the ETF matures, it will be replaced with another Treasury with the same maturity.

When you purchase individual bonds, they will typically pay interest twice a year. Many fixed income ETFs pay interest monthly so you will have better cash flow. Instead of buying just a handful of bonds (typically bonds trade in quantities of $5,000), a fixed income ETF will hold many bonds and, therefore, have greater diversity. You also don't have to worry about replacing individual bonds when they mature.

Like equity ETFs, to see the individual fixed income holdings within the ETF, go to the website of the ETF creator (iShares, SPDR, Vanguard, etc.). You can view all the individual bonds within the ETF as well as the weighting for each bond holding.

Quality Rating

As I stated, the bond holdings within an ETF are exactly as their description. If it's a AAA-rated bond ETF, that's what the rating of all the bond holdings are. You can choose a variety of fixed income ETFs to diversify your holdings when you create the fixed income allocation of your portfolio that match your risk tolerance, goals, and objectives.

Default Rates

Generally speaking, bonds have low default rates. Even junk-rated bonds don't default often. I'm not advocating that you buy junk bonds so you can get a very high rate of interest. Like most things, you tend to get what you pay for. There is risk in fixed income, even if the risk is somewhat calculated. Although uncommon, even AAA-insured bonds have defaulted in the past (Washington State Power munis in the early 1980s defaulted, and they were rated AAA). I'm not a fan of buying low-quality bonds to obtain a higher interest rate because bonds should be the stable part of a portfolio. I prefer to keep the risky assets (equities) separate from the riskless assets (fixed income). Buying low quality or junk bonds does add additional risk to a portfolio (see chapter 33).

What Does Long and Short Mean?

For a securities transaction to be complete, there must be a buy and a sell. When you buy a security, you are long that security—meaning, you own it. Also, when you buy a security, there is no limit to the upside because in theory, it can keep going up in value.

In contrast, you can actually sell a security before buying it. If you sell a security before the buy, you actually do not own it, so in essence, you are short that security. Before I explain this, I want to be clear that this is a risky strategy and is not recommended.

There are two main reasons why this is so risky (there are probably many more, but for this book, I will only use two). First, you are responsible to pay any dividends the company declares because, instead of owning the stock and receiving any dividends, you are required to pay them because you do not own it and are short the stock (think opposite of owning). The second reason, and this is much more important, is that you have limited upside gain when you are short.

For example, if you bought a stock at fifty and it goes to 0, it cannot go down any further, so your maximum profit can only be fifty. (When you are short, you want the stock to go down in value, so you can buy it for less than you sold it.) Conversely, if the security rises, you are at a loss, and that loss has no limit, until you buy it, because it can rise indefinitely. This is where short sellers get into trouble. Think about that. When you buy a stock as a long-term investor and it goes down, you just hold on. During the time you are waiting, you are collecting any dividends the company pays. Short selling is the opposite. Short selling is inverse to conventional thinking.

Leveraged ETFs

Leveraged ETFs (leveraged twice, thrice, etc.) is exactly as it sounds. The ETF purchases the holdings on margin (for leverage), and that increases your risk exponentially. Granted, it can also increase your performance significantly, but you pay a significant price in terms of risk.

I will illustrate a couple of examples for up markets and down markets using the S&P 500 index for simplicity:

Up markets. If the S&P 500 rises +25 percent over a period of time, a 2× leveraged ETF (or mutual fund) will go up +50 percent, or a 3× leveraged ETF (or mutual fund) will go up +75 percent. Simple enough, and this would be really great if markets only went up and never had declines. But they go down, too, so let's look at it from the opposite perspective.

Down markets. If the S&P 500 declines (-25 percent) over a period of time, a 2× leveraged ETF (or mutual fund) will go down (-50 percent), or a 3× leveraged ETF (or mutual fund) will go down –(-75 percent). This is where the math gets tricky, and the risk can be frightening.

If your investment declines by (-25 percent), to get back to even (the reciprocal), it must go up +33.50 percent. But if you are leveraged 2×, your loss is now (-50 percent) because of the leverage (-25 percent) × 2 = (-50 percent). To get back to even, the investment must go up +50 percent (the reciprocal of (-50 percent) is +100% ÷ 2× leverage = +50%).

At 3× leverage, it has an even greater negative impact that will be very difficult to come back from within a reasonable amount of time. If you are leveraged 3×, your loss is now (-75 percent). To get back to even, the investment must go up +133.33 percent (the reciprocal of (-75 percent) is +400% ÷ 3× leverage = +133.33%).

Consider the historic average intra-year decline for the S&P 500 is approximately (-14%) and it typically recovers within months. If you are leveraged and the investment needs to go up by 50–100 percent to recover your losses, it can take many years.

Inverse ETFs (Dangers, Especially Leveraged Inverse ETFs)

Refer to the above topics "Leveraged ETFs" and short selling.

Mutual Funds

Mutual funds (equity and fixed income) are bought and sold directly with the mutual fund company or through your financial adviser. The share price is known as the net asset value (NAV) and is determined after the market closes, when buys and sells are completed, and trades are executed and not when the order is entered intra-day.

At the end of each day, the fund manager will tally buys against sells (or vice versa). If there are more net sales than buys, the fund manager will liquidate holdings to cover the sales to be paid out to the investors raising cash from their holdings. If there are more buys, the fund manager will invest the funds in line with the policy statement of the fund. When markets decline severely (i.e., October 19, 1987), fund managers are forced to liquidate assets to raise cash to be paid out. In most cases, the portfolio manager would see a decline as a buying opportunity but is forced to sell securities rather than buy because the manager must raise cash to pay the investors who are selling shares of the fund (the opposite thinking of the average investor; hence, behavioral finance).

Bond Funds

As I stated in chapter 25, a bond fund is a professionally managed pooled investment vehicle made up of individual bonds and other debt instruments. Pooled means "it is funded by many investors and sold to investors in shares." Like an individual bond, they are bought and sold through securities firms and generally have daily liquidity (subject to the current price at the time of purchase or sale). If it's a Government bond fund, the fund would invest in Government bonds; if it's a corporate bond fund, it would invest in corporate bonds; and so on. A bond manager (or management team) would manage the fund based upon the written objectives or policy statement of the fund (in the fund prospectus) and typically pay shareholders income monthly. There is no maturity date for a bond mutual fund, and the portfolio manager will make changes on a discretionary basis to the bond holdings as necessary to maintain income and stability where possible. However, there is no guarantee of your principal investment. It can and will fluctuate in value daily.

Bond funds (not individual bonds) do not have a maturity. Because there is no maturity, your principal, or the amount you invest, is at risk when interest rates fluctuate. As interest rates rise, principal values may decline, and as interest rates decline, principal values may increase. Individual bonds also have principal risk prior to maturity, but assuming they do not default, they will mature to par value, which is $1,000 per bond (Bonds are typically bought and sold in increments of $5,000. However, par value for each bond is $1,000).

Risks in a Rising Interest Rate Environment

Bond mutual funds do not have a maturity and are subject to volatility when interest rates change. That volatility can at times be severe, and a negative impact is felt by an investor when rates are rising. The longer the maturity of the bonds held in a mutual fund, the more volatility the fund will experience when interest rates change. To put this in proper perspective, a 1 percent rise in interest rates on a thirty-year bond could result in a principal loss of (-20 percent to -25 percent) or worse. Because bond funds do not have a maturity, there is no guarantee that your principal value will be restored (see chapter 25).

Benefits in a Declining Interest Rate Environment

The flip side to this is when interest rates are high. When interest rates are high, and declining bond funds aren't bad. That's because when rates decline, your principal will actually grow. But there is no maturity, so your income over time may decline as well.

What Duration Means and How to Use It

As I discussed in chapter 33, duration is a risk number that, in its most simplistic form, means "a higher duration number translates to more risk than a lower duration number." It is the sensitivity of the price of a bond to a change in interest rates. It is also the average maturity of a bond.

When interest rates are low and rising, it's best to buy bonds with a low duration so your principal is not severely impacted as rates rise. When interest rates are high, it's best to buy longer/higher duration to take advantage of capital appreciation of the bonds as rates decline and the bonds become more valuable.

Equity Funds

If you purchase a passive (non-managed) equity index mutual fund, you are getting the same investment as a passive index ETF. The majority of equity mutual funds are managed, so choose mutual fund companies with strong and consistent track records in both good and bad markets. It's also good to look at the tenure of the portfolio managers, as they are the ones responsible for performance of the fund.

Hidden Costs to Be Aware Of

The costs of buying a mutual fund are not always straightforward. Aside from a possible upfront sales charge, many funds have additional fees not included in their stated expense ratio. Additional hidden fees may include 12b-1 fees, internal transaction costs, administrative fees, audit and legal expenses, accounting expenses, custodial charges, and others. Active strategies typically have much higher internal charges over passive mutual funds (nonmanaged index funds) because of the addition of management fees and trading costs. This applies to load funds (a load is another name for a fee, and load funds have either an upfront or deferred sales charge) and no-load funds (no upfront or deferred sales charge). Don't be fooled by the term *no-load* (no fee). Nobody works for free—there *are* fees somewhere. What is the bottom-line answer? Look at net results. Fees only really matter in the absence of value (or not getting a reasonable return on your investment).

The Main Differences Between ETFs and Mutual Funds

There are two major differences between ETFs and mutual funds. Actively managed mutual funds tend to have much higher internal fees than ETFs. As I described above, there are also many hidden costs in a mutual fund (12b-1, active expenses, etc.). But the biggest difference is how mutual funds trade in comparison to ETFs.

Where orders are taken throughout the day for all mutual funds, executions take place after the markets close, and your executed price will be based on closing prices rather than at the time you placed the order. So if you are trying to sell your mutual funds when markets are dropping and buy them when markets are rising, you will not get your actual pricing until *after* the markets are closed.

Chapter 34

What Is Modern Portfolio Theory (MPT)?

Some Thoughts to Ponder

- How would you define a diversified portfolio?
- When the stock market goes up or down, what actually is the market?
- How diversified is the S&P 500?
- If you own four different mutual funds but are all the same style, are you really diversified?
- Can risk be reduced through proper diversity?

All these questions will be answered in this chapter.

What Is Modern Portfolio Theory (MPT)?

Modern Portfolio Theory (MPT) is a theory on the construction of portfolios in a mathematically efficient manner by maximizing the expected return for any given level of risk. The theory uses a graphical plot to reveal the most desirable portfolios. For example, if portfolio A has an expected return of 7 percent with a standard deviation of 9.50 percent and portfolio B has an expected return of 7 percent with a standard deviation of 11.00 percent, portfolio A would be the more efficient portfolio to choose because it takes less risk (standard deviation—see chapter 34) than portfolio B for the same return. Plotting the most efficient portfolios on a graph and connecting the dots of each result is known as the efficient frontier, and it demonstrates the optimized (increased) returns for increased levels of risk. It achieves this optimization through proper diversification of investment styles and classes, which I will explain in detail below.

Modern Portfolio Theory was developed by Harry Markowitz, an American economist. Markowitz was the recipient of the John van Neumann Theory Prize in 1989 and was also awarded a Nobel Memorial Prize in Economic Sciences in 1990 for his development in MPT.

Are You a Fiduciary? (If You Are, This Is Extremely Important)

It is important to note that it is clearly stated in the Uniform Prudent Investor Act (UPIA), which was adopted in 1992 by the American Law Institute's Third Restatement of the Law of Trusts, that fiduciaries of trusts utilize a Modern Portfolio Theory and total-return approach to portfolio management using fiduciary investment discretion. To be clear, the Prudent Investor Act focuses on the entire portfolio composition, whereby the Prudent Man Rule requires that each investment within a portfolio be judged on its own merits (these are two very different Acts). Regardless of which rule you follow, quality is imperative for anyone acting in the capacity of a fiduciary.

Diversification

Diversification is more than just having lots of different investments in a portfolio. It's structuring a portfolio by using various styles and classes of securities that have varying degrees of correlation with one another (negative correlation means "daily performance moves opposite or not together at the same rate"). By doing this, risk is offset as all assets do not move in lockstep together.

The S&P 500 has five hundred stocks in the index (hence it's called the S&P *500*, duh). However, because the index (like most indexes) is cap-weighted, statistically approximately 85 percent of the return of this index is attributed to only approximately twelve stocks (see chapter 31). The Dow Jones Industrial index, or the Dow, has only thirty stocks. You may say thirty stocks do equate to diversity, but academics would challenge that and say you need at least fifty to sixty stocks in a portfolio to have full diversity. Then again, are thirty stocks really representative of the thousands of stocks that make up the New York Stock Exchange and NASDAQ? More specifically, there are approximately 2,800 companies listed on the New York Stock Exchange and 3,300 companies listed on NASDAQ.

Let's say you own twenty-five different stocks in your portfolio. The Dow Jones and S&P 500 are up nicely for the day, but your portfolio is down. Why is that? It's because all stocks do not go up and down at the same time. That's why having proper diversification in your portfolio and using many different styles of equities are so important. Even with proper diversification, there will be days you will not move in the same direction as the markets.

Styles and Classes

For definition, classes are stocks, bonds, and cash. Precious metals and commodities, real estate, alternative investments are also considered different classes, but for this book, we will stick with stock, bonds, and cash to keep it simple.

Styles are where we get to expand our horizon (for this book, I will only be talking about various styles within equities or stocks). When you hear that the market was up or down for the day, you have to look further. Styles (for stocks) consist of but are not limited to large cap, mid cap, small cap, microcap, international, and emerging markets. For each of those categories, you have both growth and value styles.

Cap refers to a company's capitalization. For example, large cap means large capitalized companies (the biggest companies). A couple of the basic attributes of a value company would be a low P/E ratio (chapter 34) and above average dividends, as value companies tend to take some of their earnings and pay it out to shareholders. A couple of basic attributes of a growth company would be a high P/E ratio and no to low dividends, as growth companies tend to reinvest their earnings back into the company for future growth.

Risky Assets vs. Riskless Assets

A risky asset is an equity, and a riskless asset is considered fixed income. Under no circumstances am I implying that bonds have no risk. This is just how they are classified in analytic studies.

United States Treasuries have the highest level of quality and the least amount of risk of any investment in the United States. They are backed by the full faith and credit of the United States Government. If they default, so goes the cash you have in your pocket and any money you have in the bank. However, there is still interest rate risk. That means, if you choose to sell a US Treasury prior to maturity, you would be subject to the current value. The bonds could be worth more or less than what you paid for them. (Bonds trade in the open market just as stocks do; they are subject to supply and demand and could be affected by movements in interest rates. See chapter 25.)

Even AAA-rated insured muni bonds carry risk. Those who were investing back in the early 1980s may recall Washington State Power muni bonds that were AAA rated and insured but still defaulted. Since their default, they have been unaffectionately known as Whoops bonds (especially by those who had the misfortune of owning them). During the 2008 financial crises, many AAA-insured bonds were downgraded to A rated and lost their insurance feature. Everything has risk. Some risks are very obvious, and some not so obvious. Just be aware.

Can You Diversify Away Risk?

Modern Portfolio Theory is the diversification of styles and classes within a portfolio. Since classes are made up of stocks, bonds, and cash, the more styles you have in a portfolio, the more diversity you have, and in essence, you reduce risk.

If you look at a style performance chart showing ten to twenty years of data (available on the web or from your financial advisor), you will see that styles tend to dominate for a few years at a time. One of the biggest mistakes investors make is buying what has already been in favor for a few years. That's chasing your tail and is not a smart way to invest. It's like driving your car forward while looking in the rearview mirror. That's not only foolish, but it's an accident waiting to happen. Performance is not retroactive. The legendary hockey player Wayne Gretsky, when asked what made him such a great player, was quoted, "I would go where the puck was going, not where it was."

For the fixed income portion of your portfolio, focus on quality and duration. Duration is a risk number that, in its most simplistic form, means "a higher duration number translates to more risk than a lower duration number." It is the sensitivity of the price of a bond to a change in interest rates. It is also the average maturity of a bond.

Duration can be very helpful to know when interest rates are high and there is likelihood of the Fed lowering interest rates or, conversely, when rates are low and there is likelihood of the Fed raising interest rates.

When interest rates are low, it's best to buy bonds with a low duration so your principal is not severely impacted as rates rise. When interest rates are high, it's best to buy longer/higher duration to take advantage of capital appreciation of the bonds, as rates decline and the bonds become more valuable.

One method used to diversify risk away is to buy multiple investments within the same style that have different characteristics. For example, if you are using equity ETFs (indexes), choose two or three different ETFs that have the same style but weight the holdings in the ETF differently. For large cap value, there is an ETF that replicates the Russell 1000 Value benchmark. There are additional large cap value indexes that may weigh the holdings based upon revenue, dividends, or earnings. Some ETF companies have created passive (nonmanaged) ETFs based upon their own proprietary formulas to differentiate themselves and create alpha within the ETF.

For fixed income, you can mix Government bonds with corporate bonds, preferred stocks, convertible bonds, and even CDs to spread the risk out. Just stay within the duration you chose for the bond portion of the portfolio and adjust the duration and holdings as interest rates change.

Choosing Styles

Creating a portfolio comprised of many styles of equities will generally reduce your overall risk because of low correlations between many of the styles (not all styles move up and down together). Adding various degrees of weighing to each style based on momentum of the style will also offer alpha (see chapter 34). Creating the equity allocation of your portfolio with a higher weighing toward large cap (both growth and value) will provide a solid foundation from which to build. Your financial adviser will help you develop a proper asset allocation based on your tolerance for risk (see chapter 34).

Investing via Momentum (Style Shifts and Style Rotation)

Math doesn't lie, and neither does past performance. (Future performance is not a guarantee, but you can't argue about what already took place.)

Momentum is looking at the performance numbers of a style index over the past twelve rolling months (i.e., large-cap growth or large-cap value) and seeing if the trend is rising or falling. If large-cap growth is starting to outperform large-cap value, you may want to shift small percentages of your growth holdings to large-cap value to take advantage. Just do not do this all at once. Make changes in small increments, such as 5 percent at a time, until you get to your target weighting for that style. You should do this over a period of months and not days. Don't chase performance. A metaphor I use is, "You don't have to be the first one at the party. Just don't be the last one to leave."

Never get out of the large-cap style completely. Large cap should be the foundation for your equity holdings if you do not want to be a speculator. These are the biggest companies. For example, you may have a total target weighting of 50 percent to large-cap stocks, and your current allocation is 30 percent value and 20 percent growth. Your new target weighting for value may be 40 percent because value seems to be gaining momentum over growth. Rather than moving the 10 percent all at once, I would suggest adjusting 5 percent at a time (maybe 5 percent now, and when you feel confirmed that value is doing what you expected, maybe in a month or so, move the remaining 5 percent).

When investing in mid-cap, small-cap, international, or emerging markets, invest in areas that are doing well. It's not a contest, and every style doesn't have to perform as the others. So if small cap is struggling but mid cap is doing good, eliminate small cap for now. You can always adjust later. It's also okay to have a small position, like 5 percent, allocated to a specific style. This will hedge the remainder of your portfolio and offer good diversity. Having many styles in your allocation is better than using only a few or limiting to large cap only.

Think of diversity like a baseball team. You have a field made up of nine players. Not every player is a homerun hitter or a sensational fielder. However, together they make up the entire team, and each has a specific role that's important. Proper portfolio diversification and management is very similar. Singles and doubles win more games than going for the fence and always trying for a homerun.

Chapter 35

What Is Risk?

There are two ways to understand risk and your tolerance for it. Tolerance for risk is from the investors point of view. From the adviser or portfolio managers point of view, it's purely a measurement of risk, which is mathematics.

As an investor, risk (and your tolerance for it) is what you feel inside and what makes you uneasy. It's personal and doesn't have to reflect a specific formula or what others think (see chapter 23). It's what gives you a sharp pain in your abdomen and causes stress. How it's described is up to you. It can be bungee jumping off of a bridge, or it could be looking in the mirror in the morning when you first wake and you realize you are not twenty-one years old anymore (for many of us, that can be more frightening than bungee jumping). However, it's up to *you* to define risk and *your* tolerance for it. It's what it means to you. It's extremely important to convey your tolerance to your financial adviser in the beginning of your relationship so she understands your emotions and how you react to volatility. Your adviser can then help you develop your plan and portfolio using your tolerance for risk as the foundation.

When I was an advisor, to help clients understand and define their tolerance for risk, I would use an analogy of driving to the Grand Canyon. For some, just seeing the road sign Grand Canyon 20 Miles Ahead would make them sweat. For others, the thought of hanging off the side of the Canyon by their fingernails was exciting.

For the financial adviser or portfolio manager, risk is a number that evolves from a mathematical formula or equation. The number is meaningful when comparing it to similar portfolios or benchmarks to help gauge the level of risk associated with the investment(s). I will explain that below. That risk number (standard deviation) can be used in many ways, including calculating an expected range of return.

What Is Expected Return?

Expected return is the expected performance (return) of an investment or portfolio based upon the actual historical performance of that particular investment. Basically, it's the average return of the investment or portfolio over a long period of time (typically five to ten-plus years of data) and is in no way a guarantee of future results. In contrast, if you only use a few years of data (less than five years), this number can be skewed tremendously, and projections will be misleading and not close to accurate. Past performance is not indicative of future results, but the average (expected) return can be used as a guide for projections over a long period of time.

The symbol for expected return is E_r, and I will use this symbol (below) to explain how to use expected return together with standard deviation to determine specific outcomes.

What Is Standard Deviation?

The two types of risk most commonly used in portfolio management are Beta and Standard Deviation. For this book, I will only discuss standard deviation, as it is my preference for measuring risk.

Standard deviation is a mathematical calculation derived from past performance and is used to determine how measurements are spread out from the average. I will not get overly complicated with formulas and such, and I will try to keep it simple (standard deviation is very important and worth taking the time to understand it). Good news, you do not need to know how to perform the calculation, as most investment profiles will have the standard deviation shown as well as their comparative benchmark. What's important to note is the higher the standard deviation number, the greater the risk, and the lower the number, the lesser the risk. On a global level, the number has more meaning when you compare the standard deviation to its benchmark or other investments you may be looking at. This way, you can really grasp how much risk each investment has. For example, if the S&P 500 over a ten-year period has a standard deviation of 16.20 and a mutual fund or other diversified investment has a standard deviation of 19.40, the S&P 500 has less risk. For right now, don't worry about how much more risk there is. I just want you to understand the concept. There is much more to it than just looking at a number, and I will explain that below.

The symbol for standard deviation is σ, and I will use this symbol (below) to explain how to use standard deviation together with expected return to determine specific outcomes.

Calculating Expected Ranges of Returns Using Standard Deviation Using a Bell Curve

As I just stated, standard deviation is more than just a risk number, and it is used to determine probable outcomes to get an expected range of returns over a market cycle (seven to ten-plus years).

To do this, you start by creating a bell curve to see this range of expected returns. Rather than trying to impress you with bell curves and other things you probably aren't interested in and add confusion that's not necessary, let's just use the math in a simple format. (If you are bored and have nothing better to do, you can transpose the information to a bell curve. But it will not change the result and is strictly visual if you want to impress your friends.)

To get started, take the average historic return of the investment you are looking at. For this example, let's use the S&P 500 over a ten-year period.

The S&P 500 has an expected return (Er) of 10.41 and a standard deviation (σ) of 18.39.

Add two standard deviations (to see the potential upside), and subtract two standard deviations (to see the potential downside). This will give you your expected range of returns.

Er 10.41 + σ 18.39 + σ 18.39 = +47.19

Er 10.41 - σ 18.39 - σ 18.39 = (-26.37)

Using this example would give you an expected range of returns of (-26.37%) - (+47.19%).

Using two standard deviations plus or minus will statistically result in a range of returns that will occur 95 percent of the time. In other words, you have a 5 percent chance of doing better than +47.19 percent and a 5 percent chance of doing worse than (-26.37%) in any given year.

Before you only look at the upside and get excited, just know that meteorologists use the same two standard deviations to predict weather (and you know how their predictions turn out sometimes). Also, where there are upside possibilities, downside potential exists as well.

Let's take it one step further. Let's say you are comparing two similar diversified portfolios to determine which one may be best for you. The numbers and results I am using are real (but dated). Since I'm not suggesting or recommending any investments, I will not say what each investment is. Each investment portfolio has an allocation of 65 percent equities and 35 percent fixed income.

Here is the data from the two profiles (using ten years of data):

Investment Portfolio A

Er of 8.40 and a standard deviation σ of 12.40

Er 8.40 + σ 12.40 + σ 12.40 = +33.20

Er 8.40 - σ 12.40 - σ 12.40 = (-16.40)

Using this example would give you an expected range of returns of (-16.40%) - (+33.20%).

Investment Portfolio B

Er of 7.90 and a standard deviation σ of 8.40

Er 7.90 + σ 8.40 + σ 8.40 = +24.70

Er 7.90 - σ 8.40 - σ 8.40 = (-8.90)

Using this example would give you an expected range of returns of (-8.90%) - (+24.70%).

Based upon your threshold for risk, either could be suitable. But always dig deeper before you commit your dollars. Upside performance is easy to accept. However, you may have to sit through a lousy dinner at a friend's house if you want to eat the fantastic dessert you brought. Don't be swayed by the upside returns without considering the downside performance. Look beyond the expected range of returns.

Here are just a few of the areas you may also want to look at:

- Best quarter for each portfolio
- Worst quarter for each portfolio
- Largest decline for each portfolio
- Worst four consecutive quarters for each portfolio
- Number of quarters to recover from the largest decline for each portfolio

So let's go back to each investment portfolio and look at some additional data.

Investment Portfolio A

This investment has an expected range of returns of (-16.40%) - (+33.20%).

Best quarter = +13.50%

Worst quarter = (-15.80%)

Largest decline = (-20.50%)

Worst four consecutive quarters = (-20.50%)

Number of quarters to recover from the largest decline = 3

Investment Portfolio B

This investment has an expected range of returns of (-8.90%) - (+24.70%).

Best quarter = +8.60%

Worst quarter = (-9.20%)

Largest decline = (-18.40%)

Worst 4 consecutive quarters = (-18.40%)

Number of quarters to recover from the largest decline = 4

Without sounding pessimistic, focus on the negative numbers. If you can get through the bad times, you are more likely to be invested for the good times. If you are looking for me to give you the answer as to which to choose, sorry, I will not do that. Remember, I am not offering advice. However, I am offering tools to help you make informed decisions. Sometimes, when you only look at a few things, the investment can look better or worse than it actually is. Take the time to understand the variables. You worked hard for your money, and you should reap the benefits of making good planning choices.

What is a P/E Ratio?

A P/E Ratio is the price earnings ratio of a company (or an index using the average of all P/Es within the index, such as the S&P 500). To get the current P/E ratio, simply divide the earnings into the current price per share of the stock. This number is also called a P/E multiple. You can get the projected P/E of the company by doing the same calculation using projected earnings. Some would consider using a P/E ratio to determine if a stock is overvalued or undervalued. Don't be fooled by just looking at the P/E number without understanding what the investment style of the company is.

For instance, growth companies traditionally tend to have higher P/E ratios (they reinvest their earnings back into the company for future growth), and value companies traditionally have lower P/Es (they tend to pay out part of their earnings by way of dividends to the shareholders). To determine if a P/E is high or low, you should compare it to the respective benchmark and other companies with the same style (see chapter 33, which covers styles and classes).

Creating Alpha

Alpha is also known as excess return. It's the active return on a portfolio and the value added a portfolio manager provides to generate excess returns. Alpha does not have to be a very large number to be good. Any alpha is good because it's a return in excess of its benchmark. You also have to evaluate the overall risk taken to achieve the return. Think of it this way: The difference between a gold and silver medalist in the Olympics is typically a fraction of a second. That small difference is alpha.

Alpha is not only a component of performance. It's also the value added an investment advisor or portfolio manager provides. Many investors get hung up on fees. Without making this a debate on what would be considered a fair fee, think of it this way: "A fee is high in the absence of value. Value is alpha. It's not just about performance. It's a relationship based upon trust and integrity, and having peace of mind." Alpha comes in many different ways.

Performance Measurement in Good and Bad Markets

Don't just focus on positive performance without looking at potential downside. Investing is a lifelong endeavor (see chapter 12). Take the time to know what you are investing in.

Chapter 36

Probabilistic Forecasting; aka Monte Carlo Analysis

Monte Carlo Analysis is also known as probabilistic forecasting, or random sampling analysis. The *'modern'* version of this analytical method was invented in the 1940's by Stanislaw Ulam while he was working on various nuclear weapons projects. After Ulam's method was developed, John von Neumann programmed the ENIAC computer at the Los Alamos National Laboratory to do Monte Carlo calculations and physicists there worked feverishly to determine outcomes of radiation and neutron experimentation. Using conventional deterministic mathematical methods, the physicists were still unable to solve and Ulam introduced the idea of using random sampling. The Monte Carlo method was central for the simulations needed for the Manhattan Project.

The Manhattan Project was a code name to develop an atom bomb in 1942 and came to fruition in 1945 with the detonation of the first nuclear weapon in New Mexico. It was this project that produced the first nuclear weapons during World War II.

BRAD GOLDFARB, CIMA®

It was called Monte Carlo Analysis because its inventor was a fan and frequent visitor of the Monte Carlo casinos, and unlike the reference to its name, is not really a tool for gambling. Basically, the simulations are used to model the probability of various outcomes that otherwise could not be easily predicted. It uses the impact of risk and uncertainty to forecast various outcome scenarios that are statistical in nature. What's interesting is that aside from being used in physics experiments as described above, it is also used to determine traffic flow on highways, the evolution of stars (*not to be confused with Hollywood stars*), and predict wealth from investing in the stock market. Although these predictions are scientific and created from statistical data, please don't use the predictions as a suggested guarantee in any way. They are NOT, and should be used as a guideline. I would also suggest re-running the analysis once a year to determine a pattern for future success. The future success is also attributed to staying the course with the plan you create and not timing markets.

Monte Carlo Analysis will help determine if you are on track to reach your goals, and illustrate if you can potentially run out of money during retirement. Your financial advisor can add value by creating this report and guiding you with a proper asset allocation and risk model to help you achieve your goals.

Historically, the software to create the analysis used as much past data as possible *(75 - 100 years of stock market results)*. Because of the massive volatility in the financial markets since the technology bubble in 2000, and again in 2008 during the financial crises, many of the programs are using the most recent 25 years of data. It's much more realistic and predictable *(it's always best to expect less return and hopefully get better results)*. Long term *(75-100 years)* historical returns for the market have been approximately +10% annu-

200

ally *(100% equity)*. Using the most recent 25 years (ending in 2020), that number is reduced to an annual performance that is significantly less. The past 25 years have shown average annual returns closer to the +5-7% range; a radical difference to the historical performance numbers used prior to 2000.

Here's a metaphor on how the analysis is done:

If you are using 25 years of most recent data, as described above, get 25 ping pong balls and on each one write the year and performance for that year. Then put all 25 balls into a *'bingo'* machine and mix them up. Draw the balls one at a time and list the performance for each ball as they come out until all 25 balls are removed. Now do that same exercise 3000 times and calculate the averages *(years ago, they used to perform 10,000 samplings, but found there isn't much difference in the results from using 3000 samplings)*. Think of a coin flip. You have a 50/50 chance of landing on heads, and even if the first 25 times the coin lands on tails, it soon has to go the other way and eventually it will even out. It's just statistics, and numbers don't lie!

When creating a Monte Carlo analysis, you typically use what is called *'confidence intervals'* to determine your success or outcome. Rather than try to impress you with verbiage that makes no sense, we will refer to them as the *'percentage of probability'*. Instead of using only one probability percentage, it's best to use three different percentages to get a better overall impression. Most common is using an 80%, 50% and 30% probability or chance of achievement.

The higher the probability number (80%), the lower the expected return will be (in other words, you have a higher probability to achieve a lesser annual return and a smaller probability of achieving higher annual returns).

When your advisor creates this analysis, she will also include in the report all of the inputs used so you can see how the actual portfolio outcome values were derived (inputs would include the number of years of past performance used, average annual returns, risk/standard deviation and asset allocation model selected; or specifically your asset allocation). It is recommended that you use the 80% probability results of your analysis because that is most likely to be achieved. Even though you may have achieved past performance greater than what was used for the 30% probability, the goal here is to instill confidence and inspire you *(to help achieve your dreams and not run out of money)*. I'm not suggesting that you do not to look at the 50% or 30% potential outcomes. Absolutely look at them. However, if you can live with the 80% outcome *(which is realistic)*, it's easy to get excited about the potential of your portfolio. Remember that past performance is not indictive of future results, so it's always best to expect less when planning and be pleasantly surprised if your performance is better.

When you re-run this analysis each year, compare them to see what has changed and ask your advisor to explain any differences, if any, from one year to the next. It may also be a good time to re-evaluate the portfolio and make any necessary changes as investment styles shift *(see chapter 34 on Modern Portfolio Theory)*.

You should also incorporate cash flow needs into this analysis. When your financial advisor creates your personal analysis, she will input a start date to take distributions *(possibly at an expected retirement age)* and will also add inflation annually to adjust your distributions accordingly *(you will need to take more money in future years just to keep up as buying power will change with inflation).* These distributions will impact how long your money will last as market returns fluctuate. Remember, the goal is NOT to run out of money during retirement. It's also not about trying to get the highest returns for bragging rights to your golf buddies – it should be about having the confidence to know you can retire comfortably and enjoy the benefits of all of your years of hard work.

Use Monte Carlo Analysis as a tool to help determine if your money will last throughout retirement (as long as your cash flow needs do not exceed what you stated in your input to create the analysis). It may also demonstrate that you need to reduce future spending or wait a few extra years to save more before you decide to retire.

Confidence will also help inspire you to stay with the plan you created regardless of current stock market conditions. As you read through this book, you can clearly see that most goals are shattered not because of downturns in the market, which is normal, but fear which causes you to make emotional decisions that result in getting out of the market at precisely the wrong time. Market timing does not work consistently. Even a broken clock is right twice a day. Never confuse luck with skill.

Remember, the output from this analysis will change as the financial markets constantly adjust, so it's important to do this at least annually to make sure you are still on track to reach your goals. Your results will adjust based upon any radical current market conditions and possibly changes to your asset allocation as your tolerance for risk changes as you age.

If used properly, Monte Carlo Analysis can help you stay on track to achieve your goals and with guidance from your financial advisor, alert you to adjust your portfolio allocation and/or spending as needed to stay confident in your planning.

Chapter 37

Taking Income: How to Enjoy Your Money After All of Your Hard Work

After many years of investing (and possibly having additional funds from downsizing their home), many investors reach the age of retirement with a sizable nest egg. It seems as though the possibility of running out of money during the golden years after accumulating such a large sum wouldn't exist. The sad fact is, that possibility does exist, and it happens more often that you would think.

To avoid the possibility of not having enough money to enjoy during your retirement takes careful planning. Warning: It may be difficult to stick with your plan at times. After all, how could it hurt to help the kids or grandchildren with some cash needs? Isn't that what the money is for?

Creating a Real Cash Flow Statement

A good plan begins with creating a *real* cash flow statement (see my flow statement at the end of this chapter). Most cash flow statements are fairly basic. That's where the problem begins. Cash flow statements generally do not include the expenses that may seem trivial, such as gifts, dry cleaning, hair and nails, pet boarding, cash for gambling on the golf course, haircuts and cosmetics, copayments for health care, etc. The truth is, it's these expenses that really eat away your money. If you have young kids or grandchildren and you attend many celebrations during the year, you know how the cost of gifts can really add up. What about holiday gifts? What about unplanned expenses that seem to happen annually, like buying a new television, couch, or other furnishings?

Adding a buffer or slush fund each year to your cash flow statement will avoid the added stress when these expenses show up unexpectedly. If you plan for a storm but the storm doesn't happen, you have extra food and water. Isn't that better than not being able to eat because you didn't plan for the storm?

Does Income Have to Come from Bonds Only?

When interest rates were "normal," it was expected that your income would come from your fixed income holdings. (Is there really such a thing as "normal" anymore? The 1970s saw US Treasury bond yields of 15 percent plus, and during the financial crises of 2008, we saw rates close to 0 percent.) Rates on the ten-year treasury continued to stay below 3 percent through 2019. During my career

(1985–2020), a typical annual yield on the ten-year US Treasury was between 4–6 percent.

When you get decent fixed income rates (with low risk), you can do your cash flow planning from interest only and not have to worry about tapping into your principal. When rates are low (below 4.00 percent—I will explain this below), your paradigm must change, and you should take the distributions for cash flow from the entire portfolio and not just the bond portion.

Instead of taking the distributions monthly as needed, it's best to take them quarterly or semiannually. Why? When you take money from your portfolio every month to pay your bills, you feel poor (regardless of how much your total portfolio value is). Clients with $5 million–$10 million told me they felt poor when they took funds to pay bills as needed and didn't have additional cash available. It's psychological. When you have cash on hand to cover your cash flow needs for months at a time, you do not worry about what is happening in the financial markets each day because you are not constantly raising cash from your investments. You will have less stress because nobody likes taking money out of the market, because you have to when the market is down. It's also wise to calculate your cash flow needs for an entire year and then divide that number by twelve (months) and make that number your monthly cash flow need. This way, you are funding all expenses monthly (even if you do not need that much money each month) and will not feel the impact of large expenses you pay semiannually or annually, such as car insurance or real estate taxes.

Reasonable Distribution Rates to Avoid Running Out of Money (Overspending)

It is highly advisable to keep your annual spending to 4 percent or less of your investable assets. (This is the distribution amount used when you retire, and it is based on the *assets* you have at retirement. You can increase this amount annually for inflation. See chapter 22).

Limiting your annual distributions to under 4 percent of your investable assets will give you a 95 percent chance of not running out of money during your lifetime. Investable assets do *not* include your home, cars, jewelry, clothing, artwork, and anything else outside of cash and liquid investments (see chapter 29 on reverse mortgages if most of your net worth is tied up in the equity of your home).

For example, if your investments are $1 million at the time of your retirement, you must limit your spending to 4 percent annually or $40,000; if inflation is 2.50 percent the following year, you can take $41,000 ($40,000 + 2.50% = $41,000); and so on. (Fact: Where taking a 4 percent [or less] annual distribution gives you a 95 percent chance of *not* running out of money, increasing that amount to 5 percent annually gives you an 85 percent chance of running out of money.)

To be clear, taking a 4 percent distribution annually doesn't mean you will not go into your principal when financial markets experience severe downturns and volatility. It means you have a 95 percent chance of not running out of money.

What Is Sequence of Distributions

Sequence of distributions is when you start taking money from your portfolio annually for income. When the market experiences a downturn while you are taking distributions for income, your portfolio value will be impacted greatly (see above).

Impact When Taking Distributions

Here is some basic math to demonstrate the impact of taking distributions during market pullbacks:

If you have one hundred dollars and it declines by 50 percent, you now have fifty dollars. To get back to one hundred dollars, the reciprocal return you need is 100 percent ($50 + 100% return = $100). However, you didn't take any distributions for income. For simplicity, let's say you took out twenty-five dollars during the decline. So you started with one hundred dollars and it declined 50 percent, which equals to fifty dollars, and then you withdrew another twenty-five dollars, which give you twenty-five dollars left. To get back to one hundred dollars, you must have performance of 400 percent ($25 + 400% = $100)! I am going to be brutally honest, that's not going to happen anytime soon. Statistically, limiting your income distributions to 4 percent annually will give you a 95 percent chance of not running out of money during retirement (you can adjust the distribution annually for inflation).

Plan for Success and Avoiding Stress

Creating a sound cash flow statement and including every expense is crucial for success. Each year, review the cash flow statement and make any necessary adjustments. As we age, our needs and spending changes. You may think you have plenty of assets to get you through retirement comfortably and still have funds left over for your heirs. Math doesn't lie, so I encourage you to follow the formula above to achieve the retirement you deserve.

Multidimensional Asset Planning*
Map Organizer - Cash Flow Statement©

Your Expenses	Monthly	Quarterly	Semi Annual	Annual	Your Income	Monthly
Housing					**Income**	
Rent/mortgage					Wages #1 (After Tax)	
Taxes					Wages #2 (After Tax)	
Water					Pension #1	
Insurance - primary home					Pension #2	
Insurance - secondary home					IRA Distributions #1	
Maintenance and repairs (approx.)					IRA Distributions #2	
Lawn Service					Social Security #1	
Pool Service					Social Security #2	
Community Fees					Alimony (Receive)	
Sanitation					Rent (Receive)	
Pest Control					Other income	
Utilities					**Total Income**	$ -
Electricity						
Gas						
Telephone – landline						
Telephone – mobile						
Cable TV- Internet						
Food					**NET INCOME (Monthly)**	
Groceries					Total Income (Net After - Tax)	$ -
Meals outside home					Total Expenses	$ -
Pet food					**Total Net Income (Monthly)**	$ -
Clothing and Home Furnishings						
Home Furnishings (approx)						
Clothing (approx)						
Personal Expenses						
Life insurance						
Long Term Care						
Medical/Dental insurance						
Doctor - (Co-pay, other)						
Dentist - (Co-pay, other)						
Optician - (Co-pay, other)						
Haircuts/Nails						
Cosmetics						
Dry Cleaning						
Pocket Money						
Children (Camp, School, Etc)						
Child 1						
Child 2						
Child 3						
Child 4						
Transportation						
Car registration/insurance						
Gasoline						
Car maintenance/repairs						
Payment (Lease/Own) #1						
Payment (Lease/Own) #2						
Other						
Miscellaneous						
Newspapers						
Cigarettes/Alcohol/Coffee						
Gifts - (Holiday/ birthday etc.)						
Entertainment						
Fitness membership						
Golf/Tennis						
Alimony						
Vacations (annually)						
Veterinarian / Pet Boarding						
CPA / Attorney						
Other						
Debt repayments						
Credit card (not included in above)						
Loan repayment						
Other debts						
(Additional buffer -10% annual)						
Total Expenses	$ -	$ -	$ -	$ -		

Congratulations!

You've created an asset allocation based on your tolerance for risk and are properly diversified. You are utilizing the various asset classes and the many different styles within those asset classes to maximize the performance in your portfolio while minimizing your risk. You understand what risk is, and your expectations are in line with the risk you are taking. Most importantly, you didn't give in to your emotions when the financial markets experienced turmoil, as you saw it as an opportunity rather than devastation and panic. You rode through the storm and persevered.

If you are retired, you created a cash flow statement including *all of* your expenditures by being honest with yourself and are limiting your annual withdrawals to 4 percent (possibly rewarding all these wonderful traits by periodically spending a little more and taking those bucket list vacations when your portfolio is extra good to you during outstanding performance years). You deserve to reap the rewards from the discipline you have sown and enjoy many wonderful years of retirement without financial stress.

I wish you a life filled with joy, happiness, good health, peace, love, prosperity, and all your dreams!

Brad Goldfarb

A Suitable Finish

As my mother used to write on my report cards when I was in elementary school, "I hope he does better next quarter."

About the Author

Brad was born in Brooklyn and grew up in Levittown, New York. His dad was a County worker, and his family lived paycheck to paycheck. They were also on welfare for a very short time.

He held many jobs during his youth and throughout college. During his senior year of high school, he worked for Sears in Hicksville, Long Island, as a janitor where, among his responsibilities, he cleaned the toilets nightly. Aside from Government aid and scholarships to help pay for college costs, he worked nights as a graphic artist for the yellow pages and during the day (when not in classes) he worked in the work-study program at the college. He graduated at the top of his class with a major in graphic arts and earned awards for outstanding scholastic achievements.

His passion has always been music and is a huge Beatles fan. While in college, he was the music editor for the school newspaper. He worked with some of the major record companies in New York City, where he went to school to review and write about their recording artists. During his time at college, he amassed a few thousand record albums, went to countless concerts and backstage parties, and got to interview many of the musicians he grew up listening to and admired. He was also published in two national music magazines.

Within months of graduating, he took a $3,000 personal loan and opened a print shop with a close friend. For years, he worked in the printing and graphic arts industry, which he truly loved. Always looking to challenge himself, he earned his private pilot's license in 1979. He also worked weekends as a ski instructor, which was how he met his wife, while maintaining his full-time job in graphic arts.

He married in 1983, and by late 1984, he noticed major changes happening in the printing industry and knew he had to make a career change. While maintaining his full-time job in the printing industry, he went back to school at night to study for the various securities licenses needed to become a financial advisor.

He started his career in financial services in 1985 in Cedarhurst, New York, with one of the leading financial services firms in the United States. After relocating to South Florida in 1993, he moved to another major financial services firm in Boca Raton and, within a few years, earned the title of senior vice president. In 1996, he earned the Certified Investment Management Analyst® (CIMA®) designation® through the Investments & Wealth Institute® (previously known as the Investment Management Consultants Association®, or IMCA®) and taught in conjunction with the prestigious Wharton Business School in Pennsylvania.

Brad cold called four nights a week, did seminars, and wrote articles—anything to meet people that could become clients. It was through his dedication, hard work, perseverance, and tenacity that he built a million-dollar practice on his own.

An early adopter of utilizing money managers on a fee-basis (1989), he became a qualified portfolio manager in 2009, overseeing five model portfolios he created and managed using ETFs. During his career, Brad received awards for consulting services and has also been published numerous times. An advocate for professional money management, he has appeared as a guest on radio and television many times during his career.

During the financial meltdown and chaos of 2000–2002, he did work as an extra in movies and television filmed in the Miami area while maintaining his role as a financial advisor. He appeared very briefly as an extra in two movies: *Fast and the Furious 2* and *Bad Boys 2*.

In 2005, Brad was awarded a United States Trademark for his investment management process, Multidimensional Asset Planning® (MAP), and in 2018, he became certified as a nonpublic arbitrator for Financial Industry Regulatory Authority (FINRA); a nonpublic arbitrator is an individual who works or has worked in the financial industry or who provided services to financial industry clients and is part of a selected panel to help resolve problems and disputes through the arbitration process.

After thirty-five years as a successful financial advisor and mentor to many new advisors, Brad retired on March 1, 2020, from his firm as a senior vice president and portfolio manager.

He is an avid golfer (single digit handicap), enjoys tennis and snow skiing (a former PSIA registered ski instructor), holds a private pilot's license (inactive), and enjoys travel and photography. He has been married since 1983 and has three children.

Brad's favorite saying is ***"Never forget who you were before you became who you are."***